Foxy Publishing
21B Circuit Street Boston, MA 02119

I0186913

Cinematic Mind: The Eternal Search

A Foxy Publishing book

PRINTING HISTORY
Foxy Publishing/ April 2012

For more information write to: Hakim Hill hakim.hill@gmail.com

ISBN: 978-0985466107
The Foxy Publishing is a registered trademark.

PRINTED IN THE UNITED STATES OF AMERICA

0985466103

This book is the product of a VS Entertainment artist
Kimo is the pen name for Hakim Hill

"*Cinematic Mind: The Eternal Search* is not a typical novel. Author Hakim Hill pens vivid imagery and complex emotions that tell a story through a series of epic poems. If you aren't a lover of poetry, this novel should still be on your bookshelf as the transitions between poems flows gracefully and seamlessly as the story progresses. After the first few pages, you'll get so pulled in to the story that you'll forget you're reading poetry.

What's intriguing about this novel is how Mr. Hill refers to each section as a separate film, no doubt as a reference to the title. Film three, *Chess Game With The Devil*, is particularly interesting as you move from knight to bishop to pawn to queen. In an effort not to give away any spoilers, the *Cinematic Mind's* "Game" pulled us in and kept us reading.

The novel is polished and equipped with a great design that allows you to read effortlessly. I would love to see a bit more artwork within the pages itself but overall *Cinematic Mind* was a very unique feel with a brand new method to storytelling and we rate it as a 4 out of 5. It's a must read. You won't be disappointed." ~Aziza Publishing
----

I would like to thank everyone who has supported me throughout this writing process and watched this dream, which I've had since the sixth grade, come into fruition:

Thanks to my makers: James Hill & Patricia Maughn-Hill
My siblings: Khalid, Karim, my other brothers Chris and Kyon, and one of my main sources of inspiration, my sister, Jamila. I Love all of you dearly.

I want to thank my other families who have held me down creatively: VS Entertainment: Manny Garcia, Phil Coyle; Noube Productions: Noube Rateau, William 'MVP' Medero; NFP80B: BTB, Ray, DJ Blackout; Tremeda Martin (Refined Realities), and Seeds of the Poet-Tree.

My Sigma Phi Rho family...UDDUP

I want to give a special thanks to my college professors John Mulrooney and Joyce Rain-Anderson. When every other teacher in my life thought nothing of me, you saw the talent I had bubbling inside. You never brushed me off as just a kid in the back of a class and I appreciate that.

I'd also like to thank you, the reader, for without your eyes there are no words!!

Cinematic Mind: The Eternal Search

a book of

poetic stories

*This book is dedicated to anybody
who has ever searched for something
to believe in.*

This is also dedicated to my uncle, Foxy.
RIP

Just Ink on the Page

I would never be arrogant enough to force this life, which glows of a million fireflies, into a jar of pages. Do not think of this book as an autobiography. It is merely excerpts of my life transformed into a fantasy of poetry in free verse form. An outer story or, the spine keeps the skeleton of it together.

This book lives in all of us; a story written in the ink of our blood rides the lines of our veins. We all have a story waiting to touch blank pages. We're all prose waiting to be read, or a poem anxious to be recited. We want to be heard. So when you read this, do not give me your eyes, lend me your ears. Hear the story that is being told. Listen to the punctuation.

When all has been read. When all has been heard.
Understand!

Throughout this writing process, I've learned things about myself that I never knew. This reflection was cleansing and as necessary as water is to the body. When you hear these words, reflect on your life. Realize that inner demons can be one of the greatest sources of turmoil. Let these poems become a mirror vitalizing your reflection. And the next time you look into the mirror, gaze so deep that you can hold your reflection by its flaws. Let them melt into you. Become one with them again. Let them be the wrench to unscrew your defense mechanisms.

Film Listing

Sometimes Demons Win

Phrenology Of The Fly

Film 2: Three Sides To A War

Letters To Eternity

Film 3: Chess Game With The Devil

When The Castle Crumbles,
The Kingdom Rebuilds

Cinematic Mind: The Exchange

I

It began with the night flushing the sky
Blossoming like its favorite flower
Mounting
into the peak of concrete stratosphere in its sun costume
Sunrays and all

Such a perplexing paradox
extinguishing the biracial tug between sunset and day

This wasn't my world anymore
No, mine didn't bleed this much third-world blood

This city had trees twirling into derelict buildings
Windows shattered
baring the expression of common tragedies
The wingless pigeons scathed through clouds
illuminating moonlight
in the midst of a striped flesh wound sky
like a star-lit Zebra

An Amber Flush augmented in the crack of a street
detained a stubborn pendant
between the prison of its petals:
A portrait of a young girl and her mother

The pendant wouldn't budge
It was as stubborn as this girl's city

A hawk carrying the melancholic funeral of her eyes
watched me as prey
as I walked through the desolate streets
with cracks the magnitude of the distance between a young girl

…and her deadbeat father.

The cracks bled the same blood
that leaked from a young girl's legs
as a *Trojan* infiltrated her without permission
I kept walking through the fogs of her trust

Her trust: Tar black
Enough black to see her light through it

The same light that spread
throughout the rest of her atlantic city
when this swirling tornado tunnel of a street
was embraced enough
I sunk my power-surged feet into her side street
as I continued to move forward

I could feel her yesterdays
There were so many yesterdays swarming in this area

WHY won't tomorrow clot this!?

Her voice
echoing from the birds
chirped a blowtorch burn

She said, "*I regret a lot.*"
I understood

Even a steel towered spine can rattle under regrets

There were eyes embedded
in the socket of puddles wetting my feet
Each searching, eternally, for their reason to be still

When I finally reached the theater
I walked through
the mezzanine section to the mind
of the city inside this woman of my dreams,
The row of seats split open and let me walk to the front.

II

It was a grand theater of magnificence
She said many have sat there,
but never longer than it took for them to gain pleasure

Selfishness.

My curiosity, white like a dove searching, exceeded its stay
I needed to see her film
The screen was black hole black
Dark as infinite nights
Dark as the lightest day in a concentration camp

She said "*Are you ready?*"
I confirmed

As the theater opened, I made it inside of her and saw so much:

      Vast lakes pouring down her forest-fired cheeks
      from the pain skating on her bones

          Volcanoes of blood
          and tsunamis of wrenches broke her
          disturbing every land on her body

Mysteries, like puzzle pieces, fit perfectly together
but always missing one final jigsaw

            Films of so many lengths
            So many genres

Anger and confusion romantically joined together inside of her
I saw everything
I've always been great at listening and I've learned:

We all have a heart door
beating itself for someone to enter:

All   we   need   is
           a
           Listener

In exchange for her thoughts, I let her into mine
The theater of my mind

          Our conversation was intercourse
          Her tunnel was her words
          She let me inside of her
          and I did the same

As we began to speak,
all of my yesterdays swarmed out of my mouth
like a plague of locusts or bees
They flew around her
until all that could be seen
was a tornado of insects cutting through the sheet of air
She vanished into me
She was inside of me

She was searching for my conviction- my beliefs,
and my reasons to be.

Whenever the legs of space open up to let the erect curiosity inside,
the stars gaze extra hard watching, analyzing, but most of all
anxious to see what outcome lies ahead.
The galaxy does not want to be broken...

Cinematic Mind: Before the Lion's Roar

I

The theater of my mind is dripping with vintage
The outside is majestic with bright ornamental lights
hanging from the top, spelling my name
The ticket booth fits in the middle like a centerpiece,
holding the antique building together
with entrances on either side

The lights of the booth are motion censored,
alerted by the approach of those getting too close
Twin canines stand on both sides
with the flesh of intruders
and blood dripping from their teeth
Every person has a dog on guard inside of them

> Sometimes the canines claw at their stomach,
> ripping at the inner lining...Some call it instinct
> Not quite.

The cinema plays a select few films
In theater one, the screen plays like an old family video
with hairs and static
It reeks of 90s and early 2000 spirit
with news clips playing as previews
Of course, the airwaves hold Hip Hop in its palms
flicking them into ears, serenading the early viewers
Every few minutes, the film supernovas with brightness
and black holes with the loss of yesterday...no refunds

Memories often skip like old scratched vinyl
Often times, multiple series of memories
are accidentally interchanged or inflated
The theater, or rather the person's mind,
believes in the mix ups or exaggerations
You must be careful when in this theater,
not everything is what it seems.

II

I would suppose sitting in on the first film
would properly seat her for the rail-less coaster
that rides through the next.

> Who is she?
> > Well, she, is my *Dream Girl*

Not dream girl as in the one I visualize in my head
But the one who cares enough
to pick up the book of my life
and flip through its antique, ripped, and scattered pages
She wants to know where my dreams are
and the substance they are made of
In a sense, her exploring skin
is seeking the treasures that she feels,
for whatever reason, are hidden underneath mine

> There is a lot of searching going on
> between lovers and friends
> No one ever gives up treasures that easily
> The body is a map- papyrus skin,
> birth marked land, tattoo and piercing damage,
> battle wound anger, compass eyes,
> and tongue legend help the navigator find their way

She is not quite there yet
but my inner sanctum has opened for her
The hallow walls of the theater
are listening to her every breath, testing her humility
If her heart skips a beat
like a CD scratched by the nails of a broken stereo,
the building WILL crumble with her inside of it
Her toes must walk on eggshells
She must listen to every whisper, not every word is spoken
There are silent scenes in *every* film
so she must pay attention.

III

The first film looks like a video embedded in sand dunes
Grainy like a beach with a motion picture in it
The seats feel like 10,000 carcasses laced with steel
No cup holder in the arm rests,
just oak wood twirled like a ribbon
or a bun in an adolescent girl's hair

The lights are dimming in the corners of the large
oval shaped room as Dream Girl takes her seat
The curtain, which is reminiscent to a bed sheet
after two bodies have unified and manifested their torsos
transforming its shape, slowly opens
As pulleys are heard in the far distance

Dream Girl began to watch the film
She was slowly soaked into the screen
Her body deteriorated into a mist
like a black hole breaking her apart and pulling her in
She had the best view of the train ride.

> *The lion roars*
> *like a lost planet*
> *yelling for*
> *its galaxy...*

(Film 1)

Degrees Below Separation

Some believe that the world
is made of a million jigsaw pieces
When the picture is whole
it makes the existence of God...

The Train Ride

The doors of this train open like gates to an insane asylum
The stench of ammonia
seems to be painted on the inner lining
Groups of people are interchanged
between the train and the platform
as if they are walking inside of each other
and being transported to the other side

>Oddly enough,
>nobody is looking each other in the eye
>There is a psychotic silence among the strangers
>that screams the song of paranoia
>The travelers never realize
>that their existence on the train
>may very well change the life of someone else
>Something as simple as a smile
>could alter another's world.

It is the calm storm of the butterfly that stirs echoes here
The train, oozing with yesterdays and yester-years,
moves at a sluggish pace
like a railed snail with no destination
The seats are rainbow colored with a tie-dye pattern
Advertisements of a past-decade's products
are barely hanging to the inner upper walls
above the midnight tinted windows
The seats are facing each other,
lifted above the charcoal colored floor

>These set of travelers
>Eyes the radiance of notebook paper
>Mouth of pen ink, and nose of open business
>look at each other
>as if they are searching deep within their past
>for how they know each other

One injects headphones into his ears
The volume is on *Hear Nothing*
Another buries his eyes into the grave of a newspaper
He drinks his mocha swirled coffee
and tries to turn the wheel of his attention to his job ahead
The one across from him lets the screeching of the train
distract his mental capacity
Another in the back of the train
has a heartbeat of millipede feet
He's paranoid

> But there must be a reason
> they are on this train together
> Their souls must have met before
> and agreed to meet again at this point
> This train is a totem pole, a checkpoint
> *Memories...*

Their souls agreed to meet
Or....Their *soul* agreed
It reminisces on the past.

There are multiple stories intertwined in the body
that are played out once but never truly revisited
But what if these stories were placed in order?
Each of their existence would pave the way for the next
and ultimately create the same ending...

Traveler 1: The Construction...

They yearn for something to be a part of
These construction worker-skinned
innocent eyed young seeds
are tired of rebuilding the houses
that could never hold a foundation

Tired of being the Adam and picking out their ribs
to reconstruct homes during the eve of destruction

Tired of sticking their spine out like ladders for others,
who can't even climb,
and building bridges that will forever get the wrecking ball
Their bullet-ridden eyelashes flutter in the wave of battle

Most don't even realize
they were seeds planted in the fertile lands
of the Revolutionary War
with ghosts of another time watering their growth
Their construction

    What else can they do but fight?
    This country was built on that
    Grammar school, social studies,
    their education is BUILT on that!

The foundation of the body is bred to fight
With blood on the history books,
the teachers knock these kids over with them

In any class of any city
a teacher can be heard saying:

    "Class, read chapter 8
    and learn about the Redcoats retaliation."

It must be a Tuskegee experiment with violence
A virus implanted into these babies
They watched it grow

   ...and then there is the lack of money

These families live in Section 8
The section where the heroin(e) and her side (kick)
dance underneath the tent of skin,
The prostitutes dance to the crackling spoons
until their overdosing demise

     ...they call them hoe-downs

Playing a Hop Scotch melody in the blood stream

The section where the door can't close completely
and an ex-private's home
becomes a Salvation Army to the poor and misguided
The prisons don't rehabilitate
They make it worse
Plastering the wounded
hoping it heals over

...And (de)Construction...

Pledge allegiance to the red, blue, and star spangled...

They Wolf-Ganged an entire country
The best chefs scrambled the yolk of ethnicity
under the sun's heat on Newfoundland's hot plate
Paul Revere's song is stitched to the steam
cooked in the clouds
Its raining aftermath lubricated the lands
A mixing pot of a future dinner for the rich
seasoned with black skin, just the way they like it
It's not his fault for the food poisoning
But everything that seasons this plate can be tasted

They think they're going hungry, huh?
Well actually...

They *are* the food
The rich are the tapeworms
Whatever they eat is sucked and nourished for the wealthy
like the vitamins from fruit
The juice and motivation flowing through the unfortunate
are energizing the *Powers That Be*
They thought it was a movie
A Matrix psychosis, but the war is real
The machines are real,
The human batteries are real
just not in the *Rated PG13* sense

The *Power* gains its strength from the *blue-collar* electric belt
The *batteries*
The rich are energized

This *Power* is splitting the *batteries* into polyps
growing them into cancers to deteriorate
It is the deconstruction of the human race

When the *mis*lead become *un*done
the human cancers have nothing else to do
but pledge themselves to anything
that seems real.

...Forges Lament.

They "Pledge allegiance to the red, blue..."

There's an eternal lament for not letting bullets
unlock the door to my soul like Pandora's box
Maybe my emotions would have trickled out
along with the blood

As a timid teenager
yearning to be constructed like my peers
I fitted in like Pluto in this solar system
with attire matching a gang that wasn't of my own
My bandana was dipped in blue
My comrade's in red

The red and blue gangs
had been warring for decades on end
The ghetto's militia in the uniform of baggy jeans
white t-shirts and flags
for representation of their mini country
Martyrs were made of soldiers whose weapons had fallen
and rusted into the pavement

I wasn't a soldier
My heart mumbled with the hiss of old vinyl records
Peacefully

On this particular day
when the sky wore a blue and white polka dot skirt
A soldier from the blue kingdom
approached my comrade and I
challenging the crowns bestowed on our heads
Fear painted the inner walls of my eyes
as the enemy signaled his weaponry of fire
Ire's venom found its way into my veins
as if fear detonated the underlying wrathful bomb

I stood beside my comrade as he pleaded for peace
though our crimes had already been committed
Bullets...
of sweat
dripped from our heads
as we gave up our fake crowns
My inner kingdom was shattered

But anger...
Anger was bestowed on us in its place
as a soldier of the street
knighted us into the position of fuming teens.

> *Instances like these wrap minds regularly*
> *in a form of baggage that hides*
> *in the deepest corners*
> *Usually the baggage opens during the worst*
> *possible scenario...*

I think this country is built on gangs.

I think this country is STILL run by gangs. The Republicans,

the Democrats...Those are gangs.

-Tupac Shakur

Traveler 2: The Parents...

"*Honor thy father and thy mother*"
These words are painted on the inner walls of skulls
of most beings walking this country
Embed the fear at a young age
and the foundation will wobble in the future
like a crib with three legs
balancing a baby which rocks back and forth
Though, not in the religious sense but in a broader view

The rulers of this country are the parents
The citizens are the children
High-class citizens are the eldest children

      The favorite.

Middle class are the centerpiece
while the poor are the youngest,
they aren't allowed outside much

      More age, or money,
      and the grips of the parents' hand loosens
      The parents' names are Democrat and Republican
      Usually the children get along more
      with one of them

The cousins are the enforcers, colored in blue uniform
The pig-faced family members
always come at unexpected times
taking your belongings without telling you
Such pot-belly monstrosities
Remember to pay your family back (taxes)
and they will let you be

The parents are gangs oppressing their children
Child abuse on a mass level
With every beating the children get
they grow to become more violent
If they can't please their parents
with what they bring to the table
they will take from their siblings
Sometimes the children create gangs between themselves
It makes the destruction easier
They yearn to be a part of something
but mother and father
refuse to let them be one with each other

      At times,
the parents send the children out to war with other gangs
who represent a different color flag
They give them all the basic training
and special skills needed
and have the nerve to call it a job

          Since the dawn of day, killing has been a normalcy
          We do it for free anyway
          Add money and you create permanency
          A hustle.

What makes matters more complicated
Every four years we vote for new parents
Musical chairs for adoption
We voluntarily pursue the lesser of two evils
according to which one will let us breathe a little more

Ever notice that most are never happy with the results?
Is there a way to raise three separate children
in the same exact manner of each other
and have all three happy?

Different personalities, different methods, different results
But the parents know this already
so they keep the children separated
in their individual gangs.

> Children pay attention to their parents
> The parents have their own gangs
> The children become copycats
> but without guidance or positive order,
> it becomes anarchy...

...Paint the Portrait...

There is a lost abstract portrait of *Herman* and me
painted by my mind's Michelangelo
It describes the friendship we used to have
It hangs in the empty halls of my heart

Since children, we were distant friends:
Two small figures of similar browns
Big white eyes
and clothing a little bit larger than them
Small twinkles, like the first spark of gunfire,
hangs from their earlobes
A grand space is in between them
but an orange aura belt around both of them,
holds them together
They stand on a grayish black, cracked street
All of the colors are smothered

Our paths intertwined on a yearly basis
like comrades who were destined to fight the same battle:
A sky of multiple colors meshed together
Light orange and yellows for the sunrise
Light blues and whites for the daytime
with a bright yellow ball of fire pierced into it
A sunset, the color of ripe peaches
And a night sky, the color of death

He stood underneath the night.

We unknowingly followed each other
We must have seen the future leaders residing in our spirits:
The final piece of this portrait
In back of the child-like figures are bigger versions of themselves
faded into the sky like foreshadows
There is a broken brown grandfather clock in between us
The golden pendulum lay on the ground partially shattered

...of War

The last time I saw Herman with a heartbeat was on a bus
As children we were about the same size
But now, he towered quite a few inches over me
The Twin Towers in his legs were apparent
This was a few weeks before terrorists
flew bullet planes into his chest

The last time I saw him we shook hands as if we knew it already
We spoke about a troubled friend we grew with, Isaiah,
who went down the wrong route
On the short ride we reminisced about the summers we used to have
He was always a popular kid

Herman and Isaiah would bring me along
and include me in everything
I didn't care for basketball, but they played with me
I never had money, but they would shop for me
I never had friends, but they were there for me

> *The irony of our relationship plays in my head*
> *during every accomplishment*

The last time I saw him, he seemed okay
I had a burning *lament* inside of me but him...
He seemed okay

I wasn't there when God drafted him but I still try to imagine
The gang-related war between neighborhood blocks
were at an all time high that summer
Bandana infested parks were growing in number

Murder and retaliation were becoming weekly
He wasn't involved but he was in the same circle
Bullets do not have names on them
They fiend for death and he was the next fix
The day of his funeral,
I almost died in the grave of my mother's arms

> Though anger, sorrow and paranoia have plagued my mind
> I try to empathize with the murderers and understand
> These gang wars aren't surface blemishes

They yearn to be a part of something
Even if it is just an imaginary ownership over a street corner
They need to represent something larger than themselves

Though it is hard for some to understand,
not everyone has a god to bow down to...
at least that's not what they believe
Not everyone has a sports team to represent
Not everyone has a family to make proud
with a section of their room blaring gold
from the noosing of medals
But everyone wants to represent something great
These gangs relieve that yearning, even if only temporarily

This country goes into other lands,
kill their leaders
Gather at the White House
and raise their American flag
Innocents get caught in the crossfire

These kids go into other blocks,
kill their leaders
Gather at their street corner
and throw up their respective flag
Herman was caught in the crossfire.

Paranoia locked its fierce grip around my heart since his murder
Dreams were translated into nightmares
I still see the painting of Herman so vividly;
his smile is still soothing...

Traveler 3: The Nerve of Darkness...

This disease was a terrorist attack
Lucifer ignited on God's legion of angels
The scripture was written in his own blood
so no disciples knew of its creation
to place it in the sacredness of their Book

The title is:

The Nerve of Darkness

He still keeps record of its destruction
as it ultimately trickled down to the human race
It used to drive angels insane with its genetic distortions

The disease was airborne
forcing angel's wings to ache until they reach excruciating pain
They were forced to tear them out
like scrapped pages of a distorted book
plucking each feather one at a time
leaving them in the cloud they slept in
while blood dripped
from what looked like a bear clawed shoulder blade

As a punishment for giving in to the pain
God would banish these angels from Heaven

    ....still having the disease...

but without a memory of the past life
These has-been angels mated with humans
thus keeping the disease alive

In humans, it affects their nervous system
making their nerves chew at each other
like incest creatures having lust in each other
Over time, the human will lose control of their nerves
and often you can see them trembling
Sometimes, they even lost the ability to walk
My sister has this disease
Making her wings fail
one feather

at

     a

        time.

...To Make Angels Fall

One night when I was young
Very young
and drunk with fatigue
I heard a door in our house creak open
as if a thief was creeping into the bathroom
to leak out his piss infested existence

Then...BANG!

> *The sound resembled something falling from a high place*
> *An angel falling from Heaven*
> *bustling through a cloud*
> *cracking the ground in 16 places*
> *while light snuck through the cracks of the ceiling*
> *Feathers slowly floating into the hall*
> *Like snow flurries*
> *as if a mountain of pillows had ripped*

"*Help me,*" could be heard from what sounded like a cat whispering

"*Help me...HELP ME!*"
It was her

All at once,
like arch-angels without the disease
My two brothers and I, each from our position on the bunk bed,
leaped up like some Olympic athletes in a long jump
or light leaping from its star to planet surface

> *Angel wings fully spread in a silhouette*
> *Pasted themselves to the shadows of the walls*

We all ran to her
finding her laying out on the ground
as if she was thrown there

Years later, her fingers began to tremble
One of the lightest parts of my world
is infected by an angel's disease

...the nerve of darkness.

Traveler 4: As If School Wasn't Hard Enough...

I

Somewhere in the city
where Congress discusses education
A man who has not been in school for over 30 years
let alone a public school,
stands up and says:

> *"These kids in the inner-city are just lazy!"*

II

I remember her clearly
She was dark skinned
The black seemed to be peeled off of charcoal
and glued to her during her creation
A mannequin of hate
role-modeling in the malls of Hell

> Inside the theater of her mind
> must have been horror films

She spoke the language of *"I hate you"*
She spoke it fluently to me

Her accent made her language sound permanent
Like there was history to it
Like she spoke this fuckery often

Cracks of her face frowned at me for about one hour
as if they were nailed down with odium
Her wrinkled fingers and gray hair
chewed any confidence I had in myself

She didn't know if there was anything wrong with me
Not a care about the violence in my city
Not a pinch of halo to give about my family

Every damn day at about 12:30pm
give or take a minute or two,
She would look at me and say:

"*You're going to be a failure*"

Food For Thought:
Teachers, don't get so fed up
that you forget to feed your students.

...Flying Away Made It Harder...

When school became hard enough...

       We skipped.

Hookie parties, alcohol, and weed were weekly on the agenda
of the juvenile actors' television show-like lives

       None of us were really *that* bad

We were 15 and found a way to not get caught for skipping
School wasn't too interesting to say the least
Besides, who needed to learn Latin?

So the *new* curriculum went like this:

Meet at McDonalds

Hop on the 14 bus

Wait for that girl Jennifer to come with the alcohol

Soon enough, and with enough practice, we were pros at this
I wouldn't indulge just yet; I'd wait a few more weeks
But I had a great time watching others
drown themselves into the nimbus

I did a lot of that...watching

Just like a *fly*.

And when the beat of our hearts were hollow enough
The bass from the music took over
growing from inside of us

Stretching out...

our wings.

...To Keep From Becoming Hollow.

Jennifer had the attitude of a deck of cards
with the complications of a chess board
       Minus the Queen

The Knights heavily influenced her,
seemingly the ones who'd fight for her
       but would never let a drip of rust touch their swords

The Bishop of media had her brainwashed
making her let these Jack-asses into her life

       In her search for Diamonds, she let her Heart go
       often getting cut by some fake King's spade

One thing she did understand was this:
The currency between her legs could heal all debts

There were rumors about her ways
that she would let anybody into her entrance
lay in the bed of her body
Gain pleasure
Slay her
and leave her
dead...

       Cold.

But...

We wanted to play hookie.
She supplied all of us with the tools to banish reality
and peel our skies into the galactic abyss

       Good times come with a price

She was too poor to realize
that she was worth more than that price

So when word came back that she couldn't pay her suppliers
She was sent to a room
and sentenced to kill the roots of her merchant's seeds
With a coke line of young *Trojan* boys waiting outside of the door
    Her friends in the room watching
    and her body an ocean of *liquid demon*
She settled her debts

I didn't know this would only be the first time finding out
that the entrance to a woman's womb
could be the source of her greatest wounds

    I saw her the next day at school
    She was just a body now

...hollow.

The Growth of a Fly

I

You should watch my angel wings fly me up to Heaven...

That little corner of the street
is where I rest in peace while I watch you
Wings stretch out across my back
like extensions on my shoulder blades:

      I flap...

And fly towards all the horrors

        On track...

I stay railed as if my wings come set with wheels

        I black...

Out on these paths...and flap
As you fake angels watch me...Maybe I'm too outfield
So let me fly in peace as I pry my own feathers
like a sword outside of sheath.

          It is my pen...

I dip it in the shadows that secrete from you heathens
I tattoo my mind with every little thing that I've seen
Everything that I've witnessed
From murder tragedies to storms
They storm my mind and explode like firearms
or bombs on homes in the Congo
I watch these scenes and pieces of my memories conceive
and give birth to the beast
with wings like a fly and potential like yeast

Watch me RISE,
      with eight EYES
          and WATCH all sides
             of the STREET!

I am watching, I am watching, I am watching...

I watched you destroy the peace while you brandished yours
Blowing his brain to the wall
Making the blood drip to the floor after

You shattered his boy's dreams
as he watched his father scream for mercy
But the only mercy you heard
was Marvin Gaye playing in the background

      So you slapped him around too and said:
      "BOY, this is what happens when you don't pay what you owe!"

His father was the lesson and I watched you be the teacher
I watched you bring the book of streets to life
and be the crook of peace for prices unpaid
This isn't life...it's a GAME!

And you play it for keeps cheater
You slapped up your wife beater
I feel sorry for your kids...that's one unlucky fetus
So I fly around you heathens…

for your shit house

                is my nesting home

II

All I ever really did was watch for a while
Not much of a leader
Is that something I'd teach my child?
How to be a watcher?

Traveler 6: The Architects...

The last time we had sex
our bodies became entangled in the sea wave of our sweat
mixed with the cocoon wrapping of the bed sheets

     A jellyfish penetration
     A poisonous insertion

The pearl white marble behind your window blinds
flew into the back of your mind
The walls collided and broke the time barrier

I kissed my soul into you
My tongue snatched pieces of your rib
and attached it to mine
With each stroke,
the Lego pieces of our DNA began to assemble:

Your toes curled
The way his will when the window is ajar
and the chills play games on his feet
stirring the nerves from his little brain down his leg
letting him know to keep the quilt over him

My eye lids held tighter than a vice grip
The way his will in fear when night pours its juices into his room
Making figures on the walls
as the moon's light does a breast stroke across trees
appearing to him as ghosts

We moaned
a scathing bite across the atmosphere's neck
The way his will when horror films play in the theater of his mind
and he can't pinpoint what is real and what is fiction

When the building blocks of life were cemented enough
and the construction worker limp from the extensive session
The architects heaved the last breath of a body
in some other part of town
grasping for its final oxygen atom
before the last bullet ripped open the portal between life and *elsewhere*

Elsewhere: The Alchemist snapped a photo of a future employed soul
sending him into body orientation

He said:

> *"We're open for recruitment*
> *You're not a free soul anymore son,*
> *it's time to go work in the real world."*

...Conception.

I remember when Jim Beam and sobriety
played tug-of-war with the rope of my temperament

      Splitting me
            into two halves

of myself

Half me and half *"fuck you"*
with a brass knuckle for a tongue
and a brain liquefied into itself
               in *two*, of itself

Stubborn as brick but honest
Honest as
          Honest as…

There is a metaphor for the honesty
It just hasn't unzipped itself into the world yet.

There is a world in you
Before I unload my pollution in its skies I want to tell you…

        wait.

      Honest as a newborn
before it touches the palms of any person
        walking this planet

The dirt on hands taints a baby
making their innocence rip inside out

We're all born a product of original sin
So the problem is multiplied when we multiply
so…

abort the problem before it reaches paper
Erase it before it divides us

That was Jim Beam talking
Not me.

If it were up to me
our child would be

honest.

But honestly…

We drink and smoke like medicine
Smoke swims out of the minuscule hole I form with my lips
The brown dutch paper wrapped around the marijuana
is burning a Hitler's soul red
and being passed around like the chalice of Jesus' last meal
Talks of stress lay on the leaves outside
like criminals being put down by the police
We're beating them like Rodney King's incident
My fingers, gripping the blunt
like a mother's grip on her newborn,
are getting heavier and heavier as the day goes by.
Still waiting on her phone call, I slipped into another world…

It's That Easy Huh?

As I was telling my friend about my issue,
That I may be a father in the next year
He looked at me with a bird's side-eye
as if he saw antlers growing out of my head
and said:

> *"Man, that's what you're so scared about!?*
> *Just ABORT!*
> *I've had plenty of girls do it"*

I am crucified with Christ, nevertheless I live
Yet not I, but Christ lives in me...
-Galatians 2:20

Traveler 7: The Marriage of Beliefs...

Millions dance to a heartbeat that is not in sync
Following a guidebook designed centuries ago
by their own interpretation
Everybody is right, but everybody is wrong
depending on whom you ask
That sledgehammer of fluid law can break any confused being

The scene is set in a half-breed home:
One half has the blood of Jesus trickling through its veins
A montage of crusade history
Church gatherings
Civil Rights movements gripped in the clutch of God's hand
What began from Islamic history bleeding through African veins
to conversions into the new Roman Catholicism
and so on and so forth

Quite a few leaders held Him close to their hearts
The sanctuary was a gathering place for politics and plots
Many have heard the speeches of Dr. King while in the midst of Him

Despite any belief, this fact must be appreciated.

The other half has the blood of the Buddha-hood
No outer supernatural spirits to pray to
but the inner being is cultivated
until the Mount Rushmore inside of each of us
can be dissected from miles away
My other half won't let me cultivate this side as much
but it does seem interesting
My father is a follower of a wise man named Daisaku Ikeda

There is an alter with Japanese writing resting in its chest
My father is chanting the language and it sounds so beautiful and fluent:
"Nam-Myoho-Renge-Kyo"
He's so focused with those beads falling in between his fingers
They didn't rest in my hands comfortably
My father hits his gong every so often
I wonder why he doesn't come with us to chur...

"Come now!" My mother screams
Every Sunday.

…Brings A Trial…

At church,
Every so often, I was dressed with red and white garments
The costume of an acolyte alter boy
I felt like a superhero
Like Spiderman
performing ceremonial duties.

From the third person:

A young boy with the heart of a *fly*
holding a candle lighter twice the size of him
Beady eyes glaring through him
celebrating his tenacity to his duty
The sanctuary has colorful windows
bearing the odd visuals of past saints
Like holy caricatures

> You should see this place in the darkness
> Only the cross, hanging from the ceiling
> lights up like a lonely moon
> The images are nightmarish
> with their cartoon-like features

As he makes his way down the aisle
being gazed through like an X-Ray,
He sees eye to eye with his Pastor
It is the marriage of the confused and the certain

> Unknowingly, he would cry in his arms years later.

At the front of the congregation
he was made to stand for the first half hour
But with what seemed like a million eyes staring,
a half hour felt like eternity

It was like a trial of his spirit
The pastor was his judge
The congregation was his jury
The prayer was an oath
The choir sang the song of his conviction

> *Though a church service isn't a court trial*
> *When your heart is not in it,*
> *it may seem like everybody knows*
> *As if everybody can see right through you*
> *Often when some find out your true beliefs*
> *they will judge as if it really is...*
> --------

Truthfully, I was questioning all of this even back then
But I tried to remain passionate
This was my truth and I would be wrong if I denied it.

...Between Faiths...

Some years later,
I began spending time at the Buddhist community center:
A room full of people speaking Japanese in unison
A room full of multi-cultured people speaking Japanese in unison

"Nam-Myoho-Renge-Kyo"

The people here aren't celebrating a 2-millenia-old death
They're actually happy...too
If anything, their smiles are crucified to both sides of their faces
Enthusiasm is bleeding out like the blood of Christ
Sometimes they chant slowly like His pulse as it dwindled
They speak of Heaven and Hell...internally
They eternally search for Kosenrufu:
World peace through individual happiness
They make sense...to me
But I was way too shy for their go-lucky attitudes.

From the third person:

He is sitting in a room working on art & crafts projects
Their event, Arts for Peace, is coming soon
The rest of the children are ecstatic
He's in a melancholic state painting
Meanwhile, adults are constantly trying to perform *shakabuku*

He already had a bit of confusion leaning on his temple
Conversion to another religion wouldn't happen over night.

The constant bombardment turns him off
so the light switch in his temple is set to *"out of order"*
They don't understand his withdrawn temperament
He *over-stands* Christianity too much for this right now
But still, everyone insists that he picks up the beads
and chants with them

Sometimes, the best way to open somebody's mind
is to let them open it for themselves
Too much penetration can close a hole rather than opening it...

Even though I was interested, I was too skeptical about their ways
And most of all, I was afraid of potentially going to Hell.

...Either Castling One...

I

The lobby of the multi-towered project castle
wreaked of the same odor colored on the bricks outside:

> Urine.

Apparently the *house-less* rested their heads and bladders here
whenever the sun fell asleep on them

House-less?

It takes more than a fireplace to tattoo a home in a being's heart
Ask the poor if they care about a home when they lack a house

Anyway...

The cold winter air infiltrating through the outside door passage
permanently tattooed its chill on the metal button being pushed
signaling the resident in which we sought

Goosebumps rose from more than just the cold air
Nervousness was tattooed to our skin

After a 5-minute wait, the one we sought opened the door
He was a little over five feet in height, fair skinned
with a rat's tail protruding from the bottom of the back of his head
and a tongue that could slice a diamond

His aura glowed with the ink of 90's Hip Hop
From the baggy denim blue jeans
to the slang he spoke:
An arsenal of terms ranging from "phat" to "da bomb"

He gave us the universal sign of respect
A handshake, which helms a snap at the end
Led us to the elevator, which was a claustrophobic person's nightmare,
and brought us to the top floor to where he resided

He said *"Have a seat, I'll be right with ya'll."*

II

The apartment was cluttered with ornaments
A grand television set which probably cost more than the rent
Jesus' face on paintings, little jewels, and other pieces of "art"
Christianity was tattooed in the atmosphere

The irony of the permanency in everything that I noticed
was that we were there to get tattoos ourselves
I was 16.

> *"Umm yea, I want this scripture tattooed with a cross*
> *A regular cross?*
> *Nah, I want a cross breaking*
> *Like something is coming out of it*
> *Like a breaking point*
> *Yeah, just like that..."*

The needle buzzed like a dentist's utensil
As it pierced my skin, angry blood slowly leaked out
Every nerve in me jumped at the pain
It was a blissful pain surging throughout me

As the needle continued to scathe me, I looked up
I swore I saw the flickering kitchen light dimming
like a foreshadow…

...Or Evicting Both.

The light of God slowly dimmed around me
The intensity of the Holy Spirit that I was not feeling
was hurting me more so than ever
I was 19.

It hurt
More than when *Herman* took bullets for another person's battle
More than the paranoia stitched to me afterward

In the midst of what seemed like one hundred people in prayer
I lifted my head, which felt like one hundred pounds of confusion
Tears poured down my cheeks
as though it would quench the thirst of one hundred homeless men
My friend looked at me and smiled

"*The spirit is strong huh?*" He asked
He couldn't be more wrong

> The overwhelming feeling of nothing
> can be more powerful than any other emotion

I looked around with the eyes of a newborn
as if I was seeing the world for the first time
In an instant, everything I had ever learned about the world
flashed before my eyes
Every thought of death, anguish, hatred, and malnourishment
Malnourished thoughts, it seemed to be
What used to have the face of the devil in shadowy deceit
now came to light as a human being

> It's not always battles with others that inflict pain
> Self-inflicted wounds bring pain daily

To describe the loss of faith
would take more than a Merriam-Webster dictionary
There aren't enough words in any language
There aren't enough metaphors
There aren't enough trees to cut to turn into paper
All of the ink of yesterday and tomorrow
couldn't fit on these pages to bring that kind of understanding

      But imagine sitting in a well-lit room
      and then all of the lights, including the sky
      suddenly turned off

Just yesterday, I was a believer
Today, my faith has been exorcised
Evicted and ejected from my temple
The door shut in permanency
Bolted down as if it were keeping out a poltergeist
It was homeless

Why?
When you question things for so long
you can only force yourself to believe an answer for so much longer
before your truth comes forward

      Everyone has his or her own truth
      It is so easy to judge others based on yours
      But the fact is, not everything works for everyone.

What was once truth to me
now played out like the Salem Witch trials:
A bright light haling from a cross is in the center
of a sanctuary of people
Heads are bowed in mourning of a crucifixion
that occurred over two millenniums ago
A god that never speaks back to me

Am I delusional

                                                              or are they?

There's a thin line between genius and insanity
But even they told me to follow my heart
My heart and brain battled too much
I was torn.

        Losing or not having faith is not a choice
        No person wants to lose the comfort of an afterlife
        No person wants to forever lose loved ones
        This is not something one can easily cope with
        Imagine everything you've grown to believe, vanishing
        It's one of the worst types of heartbreak one can go through...

"Son...but son, you know if you don't believe in God
you're going to Hell right?

You're father too..."

There are demons lurking on every corner,
of every street, of every city, of every country,
on this planet, in the universe of the body
Every person has a demon
When tragedy strikes and beliefs fail
It comes more often than not...

Traveler 8: The Liquid Demon...

I

Every ounce of alcohol comes laced with a demon
in search of the closed closet packed with skeletons
Finding it is the demon's eternal search

The demon, with chain-link fence rugged fur on its skin
Deer in headlight eyes
and sewage smoke breath
Is the offspring of Cerberus

> It is an attacker instead of a guard
> Vicious teeth chew through perception
> Its claws grip on to nerve endings slowing down reaction time

When it is done
The demon relaxes in the pool of stomach acids
Sopping it in, spreading its venom through the blood stream
Dehydrating the body
Sending fake messages to the brain
Exaggerating the actions
Some experience these effects more than others.

II

When the sun runs away from home
and stars play peek-a-boo with the sky
Street corners are flooded with piss jeans
and language slurring zombies
searching for their version of holy water

The glass doors of their heaven open wide for the public
Lights shining through the tunnel of city darkness
Attracting the half-dead off the wobbly sidewalk
The broken halo sign above the doors
colored in shit brown and bad teeth yellow
shine the words *Liquors & Wines*

The cryptic bodies waltz like brain-dead beings in a vegetative state
Magnetized by the beautiful rainbow colored liquids,
        Poisons
Demons in bottles
Southern Comforting quilt of browns
A city where everyone speaks Old English
Ounces of God
They drink enough to pump more life into their Lazarus
Liquid fires

God bless the 3rd degree burns on their souls.

...Sets up the Chess Board.

When the moon was red
and my attitude was blue
I felt the need to ingest the *liquid demon* at a rapid rate
My brain turned into a pinball
racking against the empty machine skull of my head

The poison, marching through my blood stream
like an army fully suited in *don't-give-a-fuck* boots
and curse word bullet banana clips,
was intent on murdering any good intention
strolling in uniform

> *"Look closely at your surrounding, young boy.*
> *Paint your picture again."*

Dark purplish, blue hues smothered on the canvas
Small white blots are splattered in it
A big white golf ball stuck in there complete with the craters
It's a night sky, stars, and moon

Underneath this dark pool at the top
are bright white high beams extending from a year 2006 Acura
Cracked, tarnished streets have zombies on them
Same zombies that were daddy's angels
But with their wings tucked underneath backpacks
which holds their energy
More energy than they ever had in their...day
Battery packed potion bottles in their hands

> *"Take another sip...watch your world transform."*

There was a house here, a two story, dirty one at that
Now it looks kind of like the Taaj Mahal
The broke-down pillars are looking sturdy and marble-ish
The zombies are beautiful, stunning - Kings and Queens
with their makeup stained blouses and the UV marks on them

But...

Who is he talking to like that?
I know you muthafucka!
I see that spine of yours can't sit straight; you need to stiffen that up!
You can't even wear your pride correctly!
Don't make me break a crack rock over your punk ass
and ruin your whole family
I've done it before!

"No you haven't, but keep it up. We like this."

Shit. Why is the palace falling apart?
It's tumbling down...
Damn. My stomach feels like something is clawing at...
Hey! Give me the phone back!
You better come here so I can break you down like this...
Damn, like this house it keeps spinning.

"The house isn't going anywhere.
But you are.
You want to play a game? You like Chess?"

My demon was doing its job...

When The Commute Ends
...Travelers get off at the same life

When the commute ends
Travelers find the foundation in their legs
Stand on their *kingdoms*
Make way to the doors when they open angrily
as if they suffered from domestic violence
And leave their personality behind them

      They have work to do
      There is no place for personality at work

So when these travelers morph back into one person
like some split personality or amoeba sewing back together
by the strings in each of their body parts
They bridge the gaps of their memories

                  Zip up their pains.
                       Buckle in the darkness.
                 Grab the storms by the throat.
            Stuff them into their pocket.
        Bury the bungee-jumping tears
      that forgot their elastic.
Quickly grab their words that always seem to let loose
      like children in a zoo
          Layer a tower around the pride
             that's beginning to dim...

Walk through the sea of people
who think they're the only fish in the ocean
Wishing the day will be a little different than the last

      ...but it's not.

Just another day ticking away the time bomb detonated at birth:
The *Heart*
Every *kingdom* owns one
Tucked away in the deepest chambers
Where the Pawns want to go
    Where the Knights keep trying to pry open
        Where the soldiers would erupt if they could
           Where the Queens wish they could live.

It ticks...

    ...until it *erupts*.

Sometimes Demons Win

We burn a Hell in the same world dealing with our separate devils

Supernova

I

Between the framed horizon
of two soaring buildings
stiff rooted
into a cement covered earth
A sun crawls up a vacant canvas sky
Like the spider in the water spout
Like smothered paint
off the dragged fingers
of a two year-old's first portrait

Rays protruding from the side
carry it upward
with a slow curve
to the globe's equinox
It pastes its conceited shine
to the buildings soul baring windows
with a stiff umbilical connection

Hands of the towers
grab the suns shine
machine gunning
day walkers caskets
as they shimmy
from grave to life

II

Most days
a phone call
to mom and dad

A simple phone call

feels like a thirty day trudge
across states
So many trials
but I don't
need a judge

III

Towers always seem to nine-eleven
on the night-breaking days
suns want to lay down
Relax its trillion-watt core
like a puddle

...of bodies

beneath the comfort
of their shade
like it used to
before skies
became so convoluted

IV

When suns sigh
like candle-wax does its flame,
or a bullet does
when it breaststrokes
some soldiers life,
it inhales what's left
of the debris
as the sand dune does
the terrorist

V

If only they knew
I have clandestine
unmarked as bone
departing the womb of body
Bathing in the life
of a dirty closet

Too many bones
in the skin
of sun
questioning its shine

VII

Pile up of grave
conspiracy theory of day
Roulette is the tick of time
raping its music
through stanza of cloud
While towers won't rise
during eclipse
of sun's judgment

Til it blinks itself
so tough
so bottomless
so...jihad
that it crashes
and

...supernovas.

Cinematic Mind: The Chess Table

I

As Dream Girl exited the first film,
drained from the visuals painted onto her irises
She started to make her way down the empty vessel theater halls
towards the second film
while getting distracted by everything in front of her

As she let her eyes run down the corridor
With bolt speed
She paused as she noticed writings on the walls
Eyeballs inhaling in the newly engraved scribbles

The words were etched in like hieroglyphs
She walked down the hall, touching the engravings
feeling her mind growing a siamese-split
the graver her fingers went

She shut the door of her eyes
and opened her fingers to the complexities
tracing each line as if to inhale the emotion through her hands
Each step, complicating the language a bit more...

She realized...these words were poems
When the heart and mind split up,
they created poems all over the theater

      Writings that helped me make sense of the world

She paced onward until the words abruptly died
as if to say a ledge was coming near
...but her eyes wouldn't open
She began to have hallucinations of a *chess table*

      "You want to play a game? You like Chess?"

She fought herself to open her eyes but they refused
Her theater hadn't made it as far as facing her own demons
so she was afraid to witness this tug of pride
My theater wouldn't let her see another film
until she understood where the first led to
In the middle of the hallway she stood frozen
drowned in the insanity of imbalance from my mind:

Opaque imagery of me at a chess table
sitting across from a dreary adaptation of myself
outlined her eyelids

It was another room within the theater
The message became clear as day

She had to get there

Our conversation wasn't for her to just get to know me
She had to help me come to realizations within myself

The shadow version of me smiled
It was supernova bright
becoming an umbrella to everything around us

With my demons running loose
their toes bubbled in my shoes
Every little thing I do
is tainted by another view

The Land of Milk and Honey

He was beginning to look quite goofy to me
with the clay of his face ballooning
as he blew a cirrus cloud out of his mouth
My friend Gerald had been to this land before
so he knew all of the tricks
and how to manipulate this mystic nature to sway his way
This was my senior year of high school and my first visit
I couldn't control anything

"*Float this way*," he said
as he telepathically bent the trees backwards making a path
We rose into the air and hovered forward
I was wearing boots a little too large
so they hung off my feet as I followed him

"*Bro, where's Mike?*" I asked impatiently...then...*SMACK*
A branch hit me in the face
He let it go
"*Stop being so paranoid*," he said.

We stopped mid-air
The trees magnetized back together
We slowly hovered back to the ground
as the grass blades parted ways for our landing
We looked at each other for five minutes
as if there was chained meat hanging from our necks
Then our frowns burst into laughter for the next ten

Crepuscular rays stretched through the gaps of our teeth
and shot stars out of our mouths
lighting the forest like a million Christmas trees.
I felt like my lungs were going to erupt at any minute
As if there was a volcano bubbling inside of them

We started to hover again and floated onwards through the land
"*There*," he said with cirrus clouds spewing out
while lifting his dry skinned sun burned finger to point in front of us
His finger had his infamous Jamaican ring with a lion on it
He pointed to what looked like a scene out of a movie
An oasis of a candy land:

Bustling brooks of Pepsi and Coca-Cola
      A chocolate-fall mixing the rivers together with milk
           Peppermint lollipop flowers with a snowcap glaze
          Grass of green lickerish
            Jaw-breaker Hedgestones
                Tree moss was golden honey
            and cookies were hanging like leaves
       In the far distance, an arctic mountain of whipped cream
     Marshmallow clouds floated by
Bushes with Cherry Head candies hanging from it were scattered sparingly.

"Is *this Heaven*?" I asked
while peeling a candy rainbow out of the air
Gerald let out a short chuckle while he started picking the lickerish grass
and said: "*Something like that. C'mon, Mike is waiting at the table.*"

The Feast

When we made it to the table, Mike was already feasting religiously
There were plates of small planet sized pancakes
with a constellation of toppings
Cups of river and saucers with triangular pieces of aurora
were decorated nicely with cloudy frosting

"*G-g-g-guys,*" Mike said
with so many cirrus clouds coming out of his mouth
he gained a speech impediment

"*This food is i-i-i-incredible!*"

Gerald and I looked at each other for a second
with smiles as wide as the Grand Canyon between our cheek bones
We didn't bother to sit on the gingerbread chairs waiting for us
We stuck our shovel hands into the grave of food on the table
burying ourselves in everything that was there
from peaks of waffles to valleys of upside-down cakes

When we were finished
and our stomachs expanded to the size of elephant
we sat and chatted as the animals came out
Squirrels, Blue Jays, Chinchillas, were all partaking
in the festive activity of face stuffing

We laid around for what felt like hours
Laughing at how the animals ate like us
as the remnants of the forest began to fade
My gingerbread chair started melting into an average chair of steel making
"*Guys, let's go,*" Gerald said lethargically.

As we began to float out of the forest, we heard a large roar
We looked back and saw three Rhino sized potbellies chasing us
with hunger fillings on their stomach cavities

Buzz Blown.

We came out of a hover as if our gassed feet magically went to E
We started running through the grass
which wasn't even grass anymore
Each stride we made
the grass Red Sea-parted into concrete
Each tree we passed blurred into a streetlight
Our tunnel vision became less and less vignette
Every bush we hurdled with kangaroo-like height
morphed into a fire hydrant
We excelled in speed and warped through the Christmas lit forest
As we sprinted, we looked back and there were no potbellies

Their eyes, their skin, the fire in their faces, their...
uniform,
were that of a cop
We were finally coming down

We weren't high anymore.

When school became hard enough for me, I skipped
On this day, we were dining and dashing at a breakfast restaurant
when someone called the police claiming that we robbed a bank

They chased us down the street and through alleyways
My boots and full stomach were weighing me down
like ankle weights as I cornered every turn
but I ran through the cramps as if the pain was a finish line

Mike was fast...too fast
His feet were working mechanical
like pulleys were being worked in his joints
by everything fast in the world
He made it back to his car and left
Gerald was a bit larger and fell behind
I kept going

I thought I was backed into a corner behind a house
when a cop found me after the owner pointed me out

I took my boots off, threw them over a gate
hopped over and ran without them with new energy

Mike and I got away
Gerald
who still had weed left in a baggy
in his pocket

didn't.

The Murder of Night Sky...

On the 4th, Red, White and Blue yell from the chamber
that Death sleeps in
There's something unsettling about the way fireworks
puncture their way through Night's stomach

      Piercing it

Tearing the Sky's insides into pieces of cloud and shreds of lightning
Eardrums are beat to the snare of its thunderous screams
Rain spills from its open slit crater of a gut

      Dripping slowly

Hitting the pavement, filling each crevice like food to an orifice
The bright starry eyes of Night twinkle with pain
Agony rips through them until they disappear into its own skin

      An eternal sleep

An internal storm commences when the final rush of fireworks
enter the Night's body and hurricanes its organs
Tornadoes brew in its chest as it gasps for air,
reaches in desperation for the worlds mulch toned hand,
and loses the wind inside of it

On the 4th,
the stratospheric collapse of Night Sky is seen by many.

...Brings Independence.

When Night declares independence
he crawls out of the firework embezzled corpse of a stratosphere
picks out the knifing pellets from the previous pyrotechnics,
peels out the mortar debris by the particle,
consumes it in his new godly spirit
and births a rocket of his own

He gracefully impales his waning moon hands
into his six pack white dwarf infested chest and pulls out this rocket
Gathers all who once admired his quilting calm into the cross-hairs
and launches a projectile of anguish into each body
Exploding like the original fireworks that hit him
The aftermath resembles a holocaust juggling of a million planets

     ...but in actuality

The aftermath resembled a tsunami wave of tears
washing away the debris of sorrow from the incident on July 4th
when the soundtrack to the War on Terror
played in the background as Jarvis was being murdered on his street

     ...Just after I crossed it

The rocket he launched after his demise was filled with anger
as he was declaring independence from this world
It hit me the next day as I recalled hearing the "fireworks"
steal another Night from my Sky

But no paranoia this time...
Just anger.

Dear brown-eyed boy,
whose night was taken away
You buried it yourself
The shovel is broken
How will you fill the grave?

Journal of a Thief

Year 1.
It started after a *mistrial in church*
I peeled a blessing off my skin like a dried scab
Floated to the corner store across the street
with spiders bubbling under my fingerprints

> So sticky
> The tarantula web
> within my hands

>> Anything I could sling in my possession
>> went with me back into the sanctuary

As a child, I even stole blessings…

Year 0.
In the winter of my temple
I sometimes wonder if this body has been lifted too
Stolen from *Elsewhere* from a soul that wanted life more than I did

> When I was in the womb
> my umbilical cord was wrapped around my neck…twice

Was I trying to commit suicide before birth?
Perhaps I was trying to steal Heaven…

Year 8.
Eight years after I first klepto'd
My impulse ticked to the clocks
on school walls

The kids in school had cell phones
Money
             Jewels
                          Cars

They shined a broken watt on the exterior
When their bags zipped open a treasure chest on the schools isle
I pirated through to take a piece of their shine

Year 4.
An infection crawled through my arm
from the poison in my own spider-like hands

             If my mother didn't bring me to the hospital
             I could've died

Antibiotics streamed through my veins
Flowing a river of time through my body
stealing me years
months
             weeks
                          days
                                       hours
                                                    minutes
                                                                 seconds.
But had I died
Would the time have gone to another cadaver?
Say…

             Herman?
Jarvis?

Year 9.
My *comrade* had a plan to spade money
between the two of us
He slaved…

    …I mean

worked part-time at Best Buy
and had a plan to have me come in
Steal an iPod
Walk out
Sling a spider-web at school
letting the insects crawl into the bait.

It worked.

Green Eyed Monster Dream

These demons had me feeling torn most nights
as if I was half alive and half a maggot eaten corpse
Half goliath, half horse
I was split between a Minotaur

or one of Satan's pets off its leash

All I knew was…
I was a little devilish inside

I was shadow boxing a curse
With green eyes, arms of fur
Six pack of beer chest, blood of vodka
Absinthe saliva, weed knotted naps
Teeth sneered like chipped pieces of crack rock
Breath of a four-month-old morning

And like a mirrored image, we faced each other

It felt like a fight for life
but the ticket was one's death

I wasn't ready to fall yet.

Not till I tangoed with a goddess
on a dance floor of clouds
But I wasn't ready to ball yet

So we brawled because my freedom was at risk!
My wrists weren't ready for death's cuffs yet

The Curse was upset
screaming from the mouth of fresh bullet wound flesh
I stayed silent standing still until the beast lost its breath

Then I lifted my sword like a torch stolen from liberty's hand
Struck down like God coming to take back his land
cutting his arm of to show him that this man was NOT playing

…my arms fell with it…

Wickedness!

I picked my sword up with my left, lifted
And impaled his chest with it
He screamed like lightning fucking an earthquake

…I screamed with it…

What was this!?

What did God have to prove with this voodoo wizardry?
So I stopped,
looked into the beasts eyes
which shined the color of dead presidents
and I asked it:

"Curse what are you?"

Its mouth, with blood dripping from its lips
Opened up and said:

"I'm yours."

Trojan Horse

I

As this crumbling cradle of a city
grips our newborns by the Achilles
We continue to watch the Trojan break inside of the women

> *As this crumbling cradle of a city*
> *grips our newborns by the Achilles*
> *We continue to watch the Trojan break inside of the women*

II

It's the injection of more than just semen
It's the wet soul flung over the fence
which cements with the invasion of nightmares
from the pool of night that fills the room
with ghosts that aren't really there
when tree branches mime the silhouette of a man

It's the repressed memories that are stitched to her jeans
as they're ripped off
    It's the magic...
           She learns to turn invisible when she looks in the mirror

III

As this crumbling cradle of a city
grips our newborns by the Achilles
We continue to watch the Trojan break inside of the women

The future "I *don't give a fucks*" of the world
in future section 8 running shoes racing through the uterus

    It's the cold stench of past...

Painted on inner walls, ceilings, baseboards, legs, and backs
And it seems, the only thing planned about parenthood
is the abortion
Extortion to the price of life
for the over abundance of rape at mass proportions

Cherries aren't popped they're picked
Moses couldn't split the Red Sea that stains them now

IV

I see seeds seemingly seize their own bodies
to cease these lives before it invades theirs

Babies, victims of a world they never came to
copping pleas for the crime of a rapist
A Trojan Horse,
who lacks a Trojan, of course
and acts like a soldier to court

These gardeners cut through a woman's forest
planting two kinds of seeds:

> The one that grows a life inside of her
> And the virus that sucks the soul out of her

V

As this crumbling cradle of a city
grips our newborns by the Achilles
We continue to watch the Trojan break inside of the women

So with the broken bell ringing madness
in the sanctuary of her mind
It's no wonder she may pay tithes to do the inhumane
when the product of something inhumane resides within her

She walks to the clinic with her feet
copycatting the rhythm of a fetal heartbeat

The choice...isn't always as clear as the window
she was screaming at in hopes that God would shatter it
so her voice could be heard

...or as clear as the plus sign on the pregnancy test that *she* shattered
...or the tears rain-storming the windowpane of her mother's eyes
when she found out it was her husband

VI

A black and white choice can be quite a mixed race to run
when after nine months
it's a new beginning rather than a finish-line

Does she fall victim to the Trojan Horse
thus becoming it herself, invading her own temple and aborting

...or let the seed grow, possibly with broken branches

Because as this crumbling cradle of a city
grips our newborns by the Achilles
We continue to watch the Trojan break inside of OUR women.

Riding the Trojan Horse

Whenever a woman says:

>*"All men are the same"*

It becomes a shielded defense by every Y chromosome to say:

>*"Well I'm different"*

But sometimes....
>sometimes.....
>>sometimes...

We're not.

We see a woman with a story of a thousand pages
enclosed within the concealment of her flesh

Epic poetry of a Homer riding the lines of her veins
Tattoos of stitched hearts bleeding into her arms
with a punchline of a chest

A Pantoum of her

>wind instrument
>wine chasing
>whirl-winding body

Wine chasing
whirl-winding body
wading in front of us with her

>...metaphorical fingers playing the vinyl of her swirling hair
>...ars poetica in her feet so when she walks,
>not only does her waist sway
>but each step is prose

And we want to read this prose

Yes!

We'd love to read every inch of her...

but only...

only...

only...

if she's in Braille.

The Lost World
(Beginnings of the Architects)

I

It was one of those weeks when she and her boyfriend
were everything *but* that
I guess their relation*ship* had an anchor in it
My thoughts...

Not my problem.

Besides, her skin was too...sex
The curve in her mouth was too "*I want you*"
for me to even *think* about turning down the opportunity
So before the hesitation formed,
I burned the thoughts

...that even thought about thinking them

She sent me her number through the Internet
and it ran to my phone on millipede feet
My fingers ran faster as they bullet-holed every button

II

At the party,
where the kid cadets inhaled alcohol like oxygen
We followed the scent of mistakes to the table
with mini glasses of liquid hallucination
We met half-court taking shot after shot
as if the referee of infidelity was keeping score
But we knew what we wanted
We hung our dignity at the door already

So the first kiss sealed the break in them
as my serpent tongue wrapped her god and broke it

Who knew one kiss could do so much damage?

But it wasn't just one kiss
We lost ourselves in the world of our lips

A beautiful world of towering castles
Red blossom skies and weather you could bathe in

However there was one "Tree of Knowledge"-esque place
An ocean of forbidden fruit in our Eden
It was a wretched beach of vast Jealous-seas
that held their relation*ship* as it waded

...and waited

for us to come back to reality
but we'd be there for the next year.

I was a home-wrecker
intruding when the temptations get too thick
Covering my disturbed world
with a painting of what it *could* be like

Truth is,

We're not always the better choice.

Points of Eruption.

In the dire times that anger had not subsided
When its crown lit up from my *lament*
The leeches of wolf aura tacked onto me,
ripped the *fly's* wings off my shoulder blades,
shark teeth impaled me into a wall, that was never there,
and filled me to a *point* of rage

Point 1

He keeps fuckin' with me man!

We were kids then
The evil in my face resembled a joker card
ripped at the smirk
rolled into a tunnel for coke to ride through

        But neither one of us were high on drugs

I was high on anger, him on jealousy
Our past friendship didn't mean anything anymore
His lust for my pain
        excited my limp fist to erect
It hurricane'd
        the city
in his gut
        broke the levee
in his eyelids
        He fell tears from
the tear in
        us.

Point 2

"Nah I'm not insecure, they just keep breakin' in..."

I didn't like to feel like I'm getting played
so when I read the chapter of his history book with her
A chapter they both hid from me
He remained a target on my radar for years

But one particular night...

bang...bang - - - - - "Open the fuckin door!"

I asked him to walk with me
as his friends watched

Truthfully,
it was a fight I would regret
IF he accepted the anger I shot at him

I knew better than to challenge multiple people
if I walked alone

Vexation goes hand and hand with insanity sometimes
and since I was a kid,
I would never let my fist go first
Defense was always the perfect excuse

Though he backed down
and I temporarily felt like I won
Pride had such a bittersweet taste
that it eventually eroded
quivered
and shriveled
like a raisin
too full of itself

Point 3

My attraction for her didn't come from her mind
...but nor did it stem from her physical self

In fact, it was more so her attraction towards me
that made me salivate for her
Even though her friend was someone
I used to date

> My spite always has a bulls-eye,
> a target, that will mend any damage done to me

> She fit it...perfectly

She was less than an object of sex
Less than a piece of meat for my lust
Less than a being

She became a weapon
A sword I would use to damage another
Even if it were indirect

I would never let someone hurt me
without them feeling pain
Even if it were a female

So when I had to wallow in the hurt
of her friend making me feel like a fool
I did the same back

I let her lips, which I owned for a night,
Rented like a pornography
from a XXX store,
smile back at my new female enemy

every

day.

Sometimes demons win...

Hitchhiking to Heart's Hideout

I

It'd been a few months since
we *lost ourselves in the world of our lips*
The *architect* still had not broken the gravity with her boyfriend
so I floated around for a while

...though he knew.

She denied it
but he had already heard the hammer rasp of my voice
pounding in the background
as the SLR sight of his ears focused on her voice
the very next morning
after the party

It became my goal
to go from understudy to lead act
A role that I was never used to

I compassed our world alone for a little while
Searching for the time she'd turn her then treasure
into an ex.

I dreamed our kiss into the world

II

It was still utopian
as the weather changed according to me and her relationship
like a mood ring tied around us
Through the race track of the year
we remained friends until the finish

Until then,
I'd walk the streets, alone
Never really paying much mind to those buying for attention
Love...or anything of the sort
was never my fortè

I had to locate my *heart*
which had been locked away for a while
chained in its sanctum
slave to its impulse
cocooned in its girth

I was walking the streets of a beach strip
with barren buildings
Palm trees swaying to the breeze of her voice
Sun dipping in its curtsy
to the sign of handsome night's presence
Fireflies waving to me in their smooth burn

Candles were appearing as I walked
Each one lit gracefully while I passed them
musically sound to my heartbeat
with matches floating in wave form
like the brooms in Fantasia
When I turned around, all I could see was a lit street
in the midst of darkness
The world was becoming a biracial oasis
Half lit
and half darkness
Half desert
and half city

A car dressed in....

    A *Car!?*

In the center of this fantasy dream world
where I *was* alone
A coral car pulled up beside me

The eyes of it sank into itself
as the image of a woman became more apparent
in the left wing of the car

   It wasn't the architect

It was another face
One that looked a bit familiar but still foreign
painted in caramel skin
minuscule in size
but very earthy

     Her eyes smiled at me
     as if to say *"you need a ride?"*

   I shook my head.
I was focused on the architect
but for a moment she cuffed my attention
by the wrist of its search

In the near distance I heard a building buzz
An alarm waking me slowly
blowing life into my half dead body
in the real world

She smiled and said, *"I'll see you later dude."*

As she rode off,
the street in front of me rippled
as she bulldozed through it
She tore into the 4th wall of the atmosphere
while the Sun and Moon clashed
building a light
brick by brick
cementing my eyes into a bright nova of time barriers

I woke up.

I was no longer in the night before
It was the next day

I looked at my cell phone
which read *9:15am.*

Phrenology of the Fly

The Drunken Bounty Hunter

Barricaded up in his office
imposing a half stir crazy state
synonymous to that of which he wishes to shotgun into another
with pictures of his target pinned like wallpaper to his walls

     desks

        mirrors

and dart bulls-eye

A flask, ¾ empty carrying the remains of Vodka
100 proof
The bounty hunter paces back and forth
planning on how to arrest his favorite convict

He has become obsessed.

He looks outside of the windows,
with the bowl-size of wide open eyes,
and sees the world for what it is:
A kid drunk on his own demons

He lost faith in it
Doesn't believe the world will be much of anything
without his leadership

    "Take another sip... watch your world transform."

The bounty hunter took a swig
which felt like swallowing a gallon of knife sharp regrets
He continues to stare out the windows
at the palace of the city resembling the Taaj Mahal
and thinks:

    "Shit. Why is the palace falling apart?"

The voices echoing within him is unbearable.

He picks up a picture and star gazes into it
In a drunken fit,
he javelin impales his flask through the window
and with a dramatic lightning-flash
as if Zeus shot-put a bolt
or an art community snapped a thousand pictures at once
against mirrors
over a glass bottom stage on a lake
It began to rain...angrily

He lets out a grunt
Sits his round pale body
with a tan trench coat
covering him like a book
into his throne-like chair

He takes off his top-hat
scratches his bald sandpaper head
and stares up at the roof of his office

As he was beginning to think about calling it quits
an epiphany ran though the bounty hunter,

      or the *Brain*,

like the cold chills of a freezing room.

If he confuses the convict,

      or the *Heart*,

he will ultimately imprison himself.

Cinematic Mind: Search For Understanding

Dream Girl broke out of the daze
feeling like an addict kicked out of a half-way house
and forced to indulge in the cold turkey experience
withholding the addiction

She was still in the hallway
leaning against the wall
as if her legs had given out

Once she gained her balance
she began her trek through the theater again
looking for the next film

From her understanding
There was a split
Between the *Heart* and the *Brain*

At the end of the hallway
where she had just felt the hallucination
she came across a grand portrait

     The Fly

It was a grandiose fly facing vertically,
with wings, left side of a Mute Swan
The right wing of Nightjar
Rigged antennae, Masamune sharp
Extravagant rainbow colored compound eyes
Thorax of a sycamore tree split by the stump for the halteres

While Dream Girl stared at this portrait
The outline of it began to glow
and feather by feather
it started tearing out of the wall
Flapping in three second spasms
as if it was caught in the wall's sticky paper

She walked up to it hesitantly
as the fly went berserk with explosions
She stood on her toes
reached as far up as she could
and rubbed the fly gently on its thorax

The fly relaxed
and then bone-fractured open from its backside
Like a trunk on a hotwired car
Green mucus dripping from the sides
revealed a light with a passage way
with a heavy swamp smog flowing through it

Without question, Dream Girl entered.

Roxbury.

In the morning,
we rise from our twin-sized caskets like zombies
after overdosing on a syringe filled with insomnia
We infiltrate our drawers like mini *Trojans*
in search of the purpose we left there the night before
after our daily intake of liquid Wonderland at the downtown bar
which resembles an insane asylum for the blue collar.

The bar,
where the cigarette smoke and weed make love in the bed of our lungs,
a sweaty sex of Jim Beam shots and hot vodka showers, conceive hangovers
that make any ceiling light look like a disco ball.

When we find the purpose,
gently wrapped in a ribbon of dignity just like we left it,
we snap it on like clip on ties
and open our front doors attempting to inflate the dried raisin of a dream
while the ocean of sun makes the shore of Roxbury recede a bit more.

As we pace the sidewalks
with the old gum and cigarette bud marks resembling mini black holes
in the space of our path in search of an event horizon to arrive in,
we make our usual route by the memorial with the spirit of Jarvis
that still fizzles around the stuffed bears like a scrambled soul
on the frying pan of a street preheated on "*gangster.*"

The young man it immortalizes had turntables for a heart
but like Jam Master Jay, had his vinyl stolen a little too early
Whispers of his music haunts like the ghosts of bullets that can't find their purpose
so stick around filling bodies with any sign of cavity.

When we reach the bus station
The one with the homeless lady who gives out blessings
like it's her 9-5
We enter the empty vessel bus
which fills up like the clogged arteries of those living on Warren street...
the street with the two chicken spots,
liquor store, two churches, police station, McDonalds, and Western Union...
We find an empty space to stand our cold stiff body until the bus stops at a destination
that can hold the marriage between our purpose and anything that will accept it.

Sometimes hope...
Hope is the only pedal keeping our feet from impaling the ground
like Flintstones marking our grave, or memorial, with stuffed bears
and a spirit that will fizzle long after we leave.

Knowing that bullets are always unwelcome guests
but inevitable like mosquito bites
which suck out souls making the trigger finger of others itch for retaliation.

Hope is the only petal left on our young kids
and as adults,
we know that at any given moment, God could pick that flower and say
"*I love you not*" blowing their souls away like dandelion seeds
before they bloom.

I always wonder what happens to those seeds.

Did Langston ever figure out what happens to those dreams deferred
on Martin Luther King boulevard
after a pistol loaded with suns came and shriveled them up?
Or was he left as clueless as the mothers with the levee shaped eyes
and New Orleans cheek bones?

Sometimes as kids,
We'd sit on the stoop popping sunflower seeds
imagining they'd grow branches into our guts
making us shine a little brighter
while the Italian ice truck sold us flavors for our future coldness.

And if we were lucky,
somebody would crack open the fire hydrant
with the ghetto's holy water washing away our sins
We used to hope for that...
Instead,
we receive wetness from sweating bullets
as we march past the street corner Nazis
with swastikas for pupils
concentrating on our burial in the camp grounds
behind the abandoned houses.

Often there were wars between our worlds
as Civil Rights dreams shattered in the birth of new segregation
when the period of bloodshed occurred over colors again
This time, our brothers chose their handicap
using a flag stained in blue or red
with a white rock as a catalyst.

It must be an American thing.

I imagine it must be hard to rule like your forefathers
when you have no fathers
Yeah...it must be.

9:15am (Timidity of the Fly)

At about 9:15 of most days
during my freshman year of college
my wings would flutter in my back
They would caterpillar through my cocoon-like skin
propelling me cannon to the nearest wall
one of my eye lenses could find
My mouth would handcuff
Imprisoning my words
whenever the African girl from my dream
felt like appearing in the real world

      She was so beautiful

This was during the architect and mine's construction
She became the nail sticking out in the foundation
The odd color in our painting
The one who would catch my fall
no more than a year later

      but for now…

I would sync her beauty from afar
Keeping distance in my search for something real
I'd kodak her image and hold it dear until…

Until it was time for a revelation.

6 Feet Above

...but still buried

The portrait of Herman and I
was smeared by the years that passed
The frame cracked as his memory pasted itself
on a wall of my heart
hanging lopsided and furniture banging against it
as the home was redecorated

The night in it grew darker as Jarvis was painted in

A few years after their funerals, I saw Isaiah
All four of us went to the same middle school

The last time I saw Herman
we spoke about Isaiah
I heard he was on drugs,
medicating the hurt in his life
Tinkering the locks of his insecurities
one false key at a time

And now, he'd become even more a shell of his former self
Medicine taking control of his body and speech
There was an abnormal weight gain
His mid-section ballooned

Apparently, Herman's death lit a rocket already inside of him
They *were* best friends

As I looked through the pages of my thoughts
looking for something to gather up
so I could make a grand speech
about how we should hang out again like old times
The only words that came off the brittle notepad of my head were:

"How are ya?"

He gave me a half smile
as if the other side was eclipsed by a cloud
he just couldn't break and said:

"I'm living man...just living."

Our World's Revelation

...A year after we entered.

The hybrid world we created during our first kiss
diminished shortly after we made it
Perhaps it was due to its unnatural birth
A Cesarean-section: We cut straight through our friendship

A funny aspect of most relation*ships*:
They won't move without a destination

We began to resemble a mouse caught in a trap
Cheese in hand but gripped by a vice

In part, it was my fault for just going with the flow
of a Jealous-sea that didn't

   or rather

wouldn't understand
looking back will not bring you upstream

We were just playing *architect*
Though she never quite left her last creation

   "Why are you visiting your ex's mother all the time?"

So we're in this world,
A year after we created it
Months after she closed the one with her ex
Now *both* staring at that union I was partly responsible for breaking
and ready for its revelation
A Hiroshima bombing of our bond
in retaliation for the Pearl Harbor breach
I committed on her and her true mate

But there was still one problem

there may be a world growing inside her...

The Bus Station

> *"The one with the homeless lady who gives out blessings..."*

My *comrades* would say,
"There goes ya auntie!"

Laughing so hard
their lungs would open their rib cages
to give the miniature beasts inside of them room to claw out
run around and break anything happy into something despicable

Laughing so saxophone
their vocal cords wrapped around the air waves
strangling every ounce of silence out of them
Laughing so...

I digress.

Everyday, before I would get on the bus
this homeless woman
who watched me grow up
would ask about my family

...and actually care to listen.
            Then she would hug me so hard
                        so deep
                                    so motherly

The only thing that seemed homeless about her
was her skin which seemed to get thinner and thinner
Everyday.

It was odd
the thinner she became
the tighter she held me

I never understood why

She told me about her significant other dying
leaving her homeless
She had a son but...he was nowhere to be found

Yet every time I saw her,
her eyes high-beamed
as if just seeing me alive
made her feel alive too

Every encounter ended with:

God Bless you!

The first time I saw a dream come true
The girl from my fantasy, the *scion*
drove through the 4th wall
ripped out of the closed dimensions of my mind
and manifested together on my bed
I gazed at her all night in shock
Stealing the music ticking in her breath
teaching myself how to breathe a piano's love
Static of Fur Elise resonated between us
for the first few nights
Our battles translated
into Mozart Piano Concerto No. 20 in D Minor
An orchestra of epic symphony
until one day

...silence.

Scripture of the latest Scion

I

It is said that in ancient time,
The Rakasa tribes would move their limbs
to the beat of angel snares
Often around the slur of smoke above bon fires,
ritualistic movements were made to signal the deity,
      Yahweh
It was a Liturgical body worship

Their arms, a sun scarred bronze
swayed to the wind pinched branches
Their legs, tattooed with sea creature's defense ink
twisted to the ocean currents
Their faces, freckled with fierceness,
focused on building the fire within each other
A spiritual connection
A spirit-ritual connection
Anger latched onto their sweat
dripping into the murderous heated flame
burning it enough to catch yesterday in it...

II

Have you ever heard of the girl born from the cusp of a flame
The arch of its shine caught enough yesterdays to black hole a tomorrow
impregnating itself from the anger salivating in it
The Rakasa praised the baby as a gift from Yahweh
for even in its infancy, its feet moved to the rhythm heard in rain drops
Silk spreads....

(This part of the scripture is torn)

...as the village gathered around to witness the christening
these words were uttered by the village priest:

"Yah bless the angel wings on Rahweh's feet
Enough kick to make a straight ground curve

Yah bless the moon in Rahweh's eyes
The sparkle of twelve mothers laid on newborns

Yah bless the flame in Rahweh's heart
The true fire of purification..."

(The rest of the scripture is torn)

III

There's a certain fate draped over scions
A certain blood coursing through its veins without compass
shipping its body into a country of its own

The latest scion, descendant of Rahweh
could dance a goblin good
The ancient tribes of Rakasa wrote of her
They said she will dance an inspiring dance
A dance that will stomp a heart whole again
A dance that will break a ground gold

Rahweh was crucified by the neighbor tribes for spiritual dancing
Such movements that lead to rebellion

In an apartment somewhere
Where the incense smoke brings nostrils to a new high,
portraits of a fist held strong enough to black eye segregation,
and dashikis are worn by the inhabitants,
a painting of Rahweh sits with a wall as its throne
An image of her dancing with thousands behind her in the same motion
Her congregation of followers

The latest scion, unaware of her ancestor
dances to the music of the new gods
A twentieth century phenomena that began in the park
The war within instruments brings her a new rhythm
in their ear drum clapping melody
Her movement hasn't begun yet

My Father

My father
is something like a shooting star

His deep set brown eyes hold life like a galaxy
but my father---is a star
His soul's filled with the gasoline of the world's woes
and lit with the fire of the inner city's passion

My father---walks with his back bent
hunched over with the weight of four world's on his shoulders:
The atlas—my siblings and I, weigh him down like twelve ton weights
but my father still walks that plank, brittle old bones and all

> My father is something like a slave to parenthood
> But he'd be damned if he was ever chained to the game
> You would never see my father dressed in law suits
> with a blue striped noose tie
> wrapped around his neck

My father never needed a judge to determine how many days a week
he gets to love his kids

My father, is something like Mike Tyson mixed with Ali:
An iron butterfly with the heart of a lion—
...skin like a pale panther

but ambition like the *black* ones.

When my father's in,
nobody's touching that ring
My father's a king, no wings
But still a fly devil and too wise

My father holds the wisdom of a 200 year old monk
from Japan, China, Taiwan, one of those places

I don't know!!

My father is a Buddhist
and every time I hear him chant:

> *"Nam myoho renge kyo*
> *Nam myoho renge kyo"*

I can't help but envision spirits running in and out of his body
like he channels a holy ghost himself

My father, is a holy ghost himself
Too Christ-like to be Christian
and too spiritual for any religion to really hold him down

My father's voice is like twin jackhammers drilling ear drums
chirping sorrows sporadically to the night

Immense raspiness, when angry... RAVAGING,
Powerful speech, his tongue is a rapture

A smile like a mirror in the sky reflecting sea off sunset,
my father would see DEATH before he' d ever see his son's set

My father speaks the language of optimism
Ribs rightly placed in his chest so when he breathes
his upper torso smiles
                 He's so magnetic
                     So prophetic
The wrinkles in my father's hands are like lines of poetry
and everything he touches is personified with emotion.
                     He's so poetic

Preaching pride prying parasites packed in people
Pushing each person to be proud of who they are
Because sometimes we need somebody to tell us
that we are worthy of this wicked world
And that's what my father does

He's the gun that shoots us all into the stars
My father

is a shooting star

The Color of Addiction

...medicine for the disease of life

A great demon once dragged a rainbow
through the muddiest valley in Hell
Ripped it by the threading between colors
Stuffed the pieces into a broken harp
that was wound into a sling shot
Ricocheted them into the air
bouncing them off clouds until one brave one

        …rained it down into civilization:

Deep-set galaxy brown eyes
Pale panther skin
wrapping a 500 watt light-bulb of a soul
"Light suffocating" black hair
atop a mountain climb of pale panther body

Full nelson black belt
Chinese knotted around left white-chocolate arm
Right white chocolate hand taps "fuck tomorrow" blue vein

Deep-set galaxy brown eyes dilate to universe expansion
as a clear syringe, full of gods, injects

Medicine of gods run loose into "fuck tomorrow" blue vein
creating constellations in body
Olympus wars internally
creating battles on the exterior

White chocolate hand places clear syringe
on chestnut brown table
as Heaven colored highs replace everything real
with Golden harp gates
Pearl white cloud floors

Oh God!

God, the color of orgasms and ecstasy
The shape of water
Angels, the color of life

His demons, the color of everything fucked up in the world
laughs in the distance
with eyes the color of pus
and teeth smiling the color of Titanic smashing ice bergs

This was my father's demon
By the time I was born
he was colorblind of all these things

Though he always tells me
He wasted a decade of his life

The Injection

...2 years after the fall

I remember...

She would sit at the table with her *cases of gods*
Instructions of the proper procedure
and clear syringes laid out in order

The procedure of a drug addict

Her *deep-set galaxy brown* eyes cracked like an egg
Yolks spilled with the thought of what was going inside of her
But it had to be done

With her voice shooting through the midsummer heat
like a bullet wrestling through its chamber
She called my name
She wanted me to watch:

"Just in case I can't do it myself one day
you should learn now"

Her caramel flavored hand
held the clear syringe filled with *her* gods
as she attempted to inject herself
in the leg

The galaxy in her eyes
expanded into a universe

My eyes
All eight
like a *fly*
telescoped
and sponged what just happened

Her caramel leg turned into a black volcano
as blood erupted out of it

Ironic how drug addictions induce temporary heaven
while medicinal relief causes more pain

...the nerve of darkness.

Pixels of Us
(Rise and Fall of the Scion)

Most nights
I dreamed her pixels
Particles of goddess and sunflower
Pieces of my mother and my sister
Pieces of a reason to stop searching
for something to believe in

      I dreamed her
      until she snow flurried into my bed

Then we loved each other
We loved each other hard as Alcatraz
Hard as Sing Sing

      but softly
      Soft as birth
          as a mother's touch
          as a feather brushing the hairs of air
      Soft as forgiveness

          It only took about four months
          for our Fur Elise to sing battle cries
          as the *Green Eyed Monster*
          introduced our first lies

Though we fought through it
Breaking apart like grains at every smell of false wind
The realer we became
the more I searched for the particles
I once dreamed of before

          I dreamed her particles of god-song
          but there was no melody

Just a soul that loved to dance
as if it was passed down from her ancestors
But she couldn't dance this goblin good
Her dance was just another *degree below my separation*

> Most nights
> I dreamed her pixels
> In real life, we swung our tongue's pistol fire
> Fought like monsters with green eyes
> like a kingdom with a civil war
> We fought headless in a room of knives

No more music for us
We spoke like oven door
Fucked like swords
Loved like prisoners

> I was never this jealous
> until...her

> Until she owned me dog leash
> Until I couldn't do anything
> without her thinking I was trying to slay her
> Until our lies became the truth
> that we built a foundation on

Until the words "I love you"
felt about as empty as my faith
Until it became too hard to trust a person
who didn't trust anybody

> Until every particle faded
> and I couldn't remember
> why I used to dream of her
> in the first place

But dreams never fade, do they?
They repress but come back
like I left and came back
like she left and came back
like a juggling flu
        See-sawing on a pendulum
        swinging faster than our eyes

We should've broke before
but now every tomorrow
comes laced with the sick drug
of yesterday's pain
We smoke that pain every time today
gets a little too hard

        And it is hard
            …especially when other people
              get mixed into our pixels

Most fights ain't shit
Just another flavor of hatred
to add to this plate of ours

            While we eat
            like starving fools

Knowing we're going to vomit
the moment our love tastes off

        And it is off
        as it always was

           As we fight over him
                over her
                over miscommunication
                over petty insults

But the irony of it all

No matter how many times
we died...

Like friends do
     like faith does...

We always came back
Cycling like seasons
Like reasons to stop searching
for something real

Last night,
I loved her 8 million pixilated colors of hatred
They must be one in the same
All I know is,
if love isn't eternal

then Heaven must not be either.

Snow White

...and the seven dwarfs

In the basement of any college party
On any college campus

Where the books have closed for the night
The emergency lights of hallways gently light the classrooms

Where the grass outside of a residence hall is becoming dry
as the winter air caves each bristle's chest in
The sprinklers still haven't been fixed
since the haymaker of a brick rampaged it

Where last night's stomach acids erode the ground
while the fake track stars continue to giggle and hurdle over it
Campus boars, with their pot-bellies hanging half an inch out of their uniform
switch on their lights that resemble the color of the flag
that never protects the passerby's rights

Where the twin-sized prison bed of a dorm room
can fit three bodies when each are inserted into each other correctly

Where the eyes are glued to the hue of a TV screen
while an essay resides just below it with a beautifully written "F" at the top

Where an underground flier is passed around
and it reads "house party at midnight" on blank street
You enter and are told to go downstairs to the basement
where you will see Snow White and seven young men
with beer cans broken and spilled all over the pigsty of a room
sitting around a table with white powder
being cut up into lines
While rock music enters your heart's chambers
and the bass echoes the steel bars
creating anxiety
Snow White will look up at you and say
"You want some?"

The Backstabber's Haiku

We sat in the car
speaking about life while he
kicked game to my ex

And when you leave
You'll pack your bags

of emotion

exiting stage left
searching for something else
without a clue of what it is

but you forgot

somebody has to design
the treasure map

Somebody.

At South Station

I thought my next experience would change my life

...it did.

My father and the *scion*
who was now my ex
waited with me at South Station
as we awaited my departure for Washington D.C.
We couldn't stop looking at each other

The scion and I, that is.

Our eyes fell into each other
gazing into the yesteryears of our battlefield relationship
Reminiscing on the way our attitudes would swing
like a room full of pendulum axes
with jealousy on the edges
anointing the sharpness with its poison

an eminent ivy
with its life juice
spilling from the *Green Monster's* black gums

The monster would hang from the roof
of our thoughts
Making sure each pendulum
swiped our hearts if ever one tried
to make it to the other.

I needed success by any means
even if it meant temporarily leaving her
so when I scored a job in another state for four months
I thought she would be happy for me

As I walked to my train and looked back at her
with tears filling both of our eyes
as she promised to visit me
as soon as possible
I thought maybe...

just maybe

Maybe we really do love each other.

....

In a half drunk daze
a bottle of *liquid demon*
spilled on the coffee table
filling its empty crevice purposefully
like a block of soul melted to liquid state
with pieces of 10 cent noodles swimming in it
I looked at my phone
squinted my eyes from what seemed like an ultraviolet glow
that ran away from sun and touchdown on pupil
and read the words that spelled out:
"I'm not coming."

      "Must be the backstabber," I thought.

The night slipped down
a little bit closer that day
Smiling its crooked buck tooth moon at me
Throwing javelins of betrayal through the air
like an Olympic heartbroken champ
as it combed out its depressing hair of sadness

      It wanted my pride
      Pursuing my sex in order to attain it

      I looked out of my window
      at the curved body of this new city I was in
      The streets that caressed the decay of abandonment
      Heartbroken signs, signaling the turn of each quadrant

The city became a woman that I didn't know how to love
I stole each pigment of flesh
from the darkness of the sky
Aroused its skin
and sexed to the blowtorch of loneliness

Dear brown-eyed boy,
with the jackhammer heart
nailing away at its prison
You accidently...

Re-punctured your sky.

The *color of your addiction*
Leaks out the night.

A One Snow White Stand

We were all *liquid demon*
and half lust that night
I didn't even care to help clean up
after the room quaked
from the tectonic pelvic clashing that night

I didn't speak to you again after that night

In the bar, your eyes were a dressing room
Peeling back every layer of gentleman off me
I returned the favor on the way back to your room
Our tongues gripping each other for life

      I thought I found a soul down there

When I unbuttoned who you were the day before
Underneath, I found everything I had tried to avoid in you
I licked each piece of hurt off of you
Taking them back
Bandaging my wounds

I didn't feel much pleasure after releasing
I didn't feel much satisfaction
from collecting yet another body

I just felt the after-effects of being high
as if your body was just a *case of gods*
zip-locked in this casing of pearly white flesh

My door needed to inhale you
It needed to soak you in hopes…

      that you could ring the liberty bell of my chest
      But this lust…

           …like most demons…

      was only a temporary fix.

As I entered you
It felt like an out of body experience
I floated to the ceiling
like the ghoulish ballet twirl of candle spirit

I watched myself
become just like the other guys
who I once said I wasn't
In you...

But seeing her.

Three Sides to a War

The metaphor between the heart and mind is unending

They battle each other for dominance

The impulse- the reaction, the passion

the Heart...is the beast

The brain- often thinking twice, is the logical creature

but guilty of its own crimes...withholding power

There are three sides to this war:

The impulse, the logic, and...

Cinematic Mind: Logical Impulse

I

Dream Girl was launched out the backside of the *fly*
into another part of the theater
She looked around for a moment
and paused before she continued deeper in

> This moment...this very moment
> is called "understanding"
> It is not enough to listen or read
> Comprehension is needed more than anything else

As she proceeded down the corridor
the halls began to transform
What were once chandeliers,
became clouds free flowing across the ceiling
The walls slowly started meshing into paintings
of giant sequoia trees and long bristles of grass
The portrait frames slowly faded into the walls

The further she walked, the more elaborate the painting became
There is a war
Soldiers in blood red metal armor with hearts painted over their chest plates
hide behind trees with swords out

The enemy?

Further down the walls are images of soldiers
with black fatigue uniform
In their burly, pale hands were automatic pistols
equipped with hair grazing red dot lasers
Their fatigues had a brain painted over the chest
Two sets of soldiers, bred from two different time spans
in the same portrait battling each other for control.

II

At the end of this corridor painting
laid the second film
The entrance door
half battered and pulsating back and forth
had the words *Logical Impulse* etched into it
Dream Girl turned the knob
which was half burned off
like a cigarette bud on fire for too long

The theater was desolate
Half of the seats had the backs blown into pieces
with shreds of it laying on the floor
resembling saw dust
The curtains, which were open with black burn marks on the edges
were tearing off of the pulleys

Dream Girl took her seat in the middle
in one of the only seats that were still whole
This movie played like a battle film
with a dark horrific luminous filter

As the screen turned white and soaked in a wet, enthusiastic girl
She began to realize that there is much more
than an average war within the body
Everything plays a part
Every degree of separation comes forth.

> *Wars happen every day, behind the body*
> *within the body, underneath the flesh*
> *Civil wars that emancipation could never solve*
> *The Union must be completed...*

The Heart's Side of the Story: Innocent Criminal

I

I'm sentenced for life to be a prisoner of this flesh
My crime?
Whenever the ghoulish smoke fucks the atmosphere
giving birth to blurry mirrors,
I push past the laws of the bastard logic
I push this body towards the grim black reflection of its face
Forcing the eyes to gaze at themselves
Forcing it to see a king in a corpse

>   You'd be staggered by the amount of cells
>   walking this earth without me
>   I know I deserve more
>   I only yearn for more control
>   They say I pump the cells
>   I am IN a cell

And so I'm judged against the motives of Lucifer
for wanting more power than the brain is willing to give
I'll wear that title across my tissue

II

The brain is God around these parts
He flaunts His arrogance
He walks around this old western-crusted body's ranch
with spurs on His boots gun slinging His logic

A cowboy?
Not quite.

He's a cell herder; he controls from the inside
Often thinking two, three, or even four times
sending this here body through a rodeo

On the outside, other cities, or bodies,
call ours a split personality
In actuality, our judicial state is under anarchy
because of Brain's work
That asshole can never think straight

He is the chauffeur that drives a man insane
Making one look at oneself in the mirror
yet see everything that isn't there
Often thinking but never understanding
With white face, white gloves,
and "I don't know" black clothing
Brain tries to mime His way over speed bumps
in this street life

A sergeant with twin Glock arms to control
When He's depressed,
He forces the body to intake alcohol at a rapid rate
knowing He will be directly drowned trying to swim
in the wave of intoxication

HE is the true reason for such intake
The illegal trafficking of marijuana past
border control between mouth and lungs
The expletive language written on tongue
and spoken like a Rated R movie
The obvious criminal activity

> *"It's not a mistake when you know right from wrong, boy*
> *Stop acting like you don't know the difference."*

Brain gains from this
He earns satisfaction of learning a "lesson"
even though the lesson was already thought through

HE is the reason behind the marriage of:
Butterfly knife and lower torso
Sweet hollow tip bullet and my friends
the twin lung crew

You know the smoke lingering over blunt Hell fire?
HE is the reason we have to inhale it.

When I was arrested during the adolescence of this body
Brain, with the Sun head-locked in his teeth
came in to sentence the blood flowing in me

III

He said:

"You are guilty...
On ten accounts of armed robbery of realism

For the planting of a timed dream bomb
that detonated in the core of this man's chest bank
You stole the gold-plated hand with hope crunched in its palm
We have you on camera
For the false promises hog tied
and hung between the cage of his ribs

You are the reason hope hangs
like a lingering slave that forgets it's dead

You are the reason this hero came equipped
with a knife in his gut, death is always awaiting

You are the reason for him 'falling' in love
instead of walking side by side with it
When this man fell, he broke
Only logic could have prevented this."

The broom of reverse conviction
sweeps me away every time
The perpetual middle finger key
locking my cell fuels my anger triumphantly

Brain is the reason this body lost faith
Faith isn't something you *think* about.

The Brain's Side of the Story: Sergeant at Arms

I

The problem is Right and Wrong see-saw
like a tornado fucking on a trampoline
Heart thinks he's innocent? Of course!

So did Ted Bundy's iceberg skating heart
during the mutilation of those many women

So did Jack The Ripper's plastic surgeon heart
when the prostitutes found that their final bed to lay in
was in a hostel six feet beneath them on the corner of Hell Street

Heart promotes passion
Passion promotes impulse
Impulse lacks logic
PERIOD!

Let me guess,
He painfully exclaimed that he is in a shadow dwelling cell
and how we, the Council of Logic, impede his progression
by judging him against the motives of Lucifer, right?

Sure we do!

Me and the eclectic nerve team
wrap ourselves around every loose end body part
like vines, produce the juice given to us by God
and pass it through all of them with plan and purpose

PLAN AND PURPOSE!

Heart, with the impulse of a fourth grader
being weaned into multiplication
needs me to step in
whenever he gets too ahead of himself

II

On the outside of my pale skin
I am a bounty hunter
On this inside,
I am a Godly being
forgiving most criminals
for what they do

They call it: healing

I am the captain of this here broken down ship, or body,
whatever you want to call it
Guiding it through the cracked mangling concrete
as the obstacles pop up like skin infections
I am the seer of all things

When the minuscule arms tighten with anger
I work double to loosen them up
Horses, code name Charlies, rise daily
like mole hills
I dissolve them

Heart?
He is a confused soul
An organ donor
giving himself to any cause striking a jump
in the very blood flowing through him
Let me tell you a story about him

III

Heart wasn't always impulsive
Let me set the scene:

"As a timid teenager yearning to be constructed like his peers,
He fit in like Pluto in this solar system
with attire matching a gang that wasn't his own
His bandana was dipped in blue
His comrade's in red.

The red and blue gangs had been warring for decades on end
The ghetto's militia in the uniform of baggy jeans
White t-shirts and flags for representation of their mini country
Martyrs were made of soldiers whose weapons had fallen
and rusted into the pavement
He wasn't a soldier... "

Oh, you've heard this story before?
Ah yes, a broken pride is strong enough to break a warm heart cold
His once pretty eyes, dilated an angry brown
His once warm hands, now stiffened
like clay left in the heat too long
In fact, he was left in the heat too long
He even keeps a *painting of our dead comrade* in his cell
After these absurd events, Heart became impulsive
Acting on anger
I can't say I blame him
But I must do my job at all times
My job requires thought

And so we convicted him of these charges
and taxed him to the game of life
The Council of Logic has had enough of cleaning up Heart's messes

The Reconciliation

I

Heart, with his screwdriver-like jalapeño fingers
balls his fist and pounds the shadowy chambers
of his cell whenever he gets upset

After staring at the *painting of Herman* for so long
He'd had enough of imprisonment

He rose from his cot like a zombie being reborn,
walked to his cell bars and exclaimed:
"LET ME OUT!"

His voice rang of a hundred church bells
Throughout the City of Body, his voice could be heard
bouncing off ribs, bones, sinking into tissue,
latching rides to blood cells, manipulating the white cells
Sending an impulse, a panic, to the brain
The body went stir crazy until the head began to ache
A migraine the magnitude of 7.0 stirred
Brain was alarmed at this *point of eruption*

II

Brain, through electric convulsions,
made his way down to Heart's cell

He tried to reason with Heart:
"Heart, this is why you're jailed right now,
you must not startle the city at this moment!"
Heart yelled:
"WHY!"

Brain:
"The body is at war.
Its devil's have been haunting us for some time now
We've been challenged to a duel..."

Heart cut him off:
"I don't care. I DON'T CARE!"

Heart reached his arms around the bars
and bent them like the spines of a scoliosis victim
swerving them into S shapes
With blood red eyes
similar to the glow of the moon reflecting Mars,
Skin of sand paper texture,
and sweatpants wet with anger,
walked through the gates and approached Brain

They stood face to face
Brain, carrying the calm of great seas without a moon tide
A tan trench coat, sun bathed baldhead,
and a spaced out attitude Neil Armstrong could float with
squinted his light brown owl eyes back into Heart's face
He was trying to read him...

Actually, he was trying to let Heart read *him*.

Heart:
"I know what you're thinking."

Brain replied:
"And I know what you're feeling."

The Council of Logic entered the holding chambers
in alignment with a diverse ethnicity resembling the United Nations
4 men and 4 women, all wearing tan trench coats,
stood behind Brain

Brain:

"I will take care of Heart. Go calm the city down,
we don't want a panic attack."

The Council nodded in agreement
They gave Heart a piercing gaze and then exited to work on the body's nerves
Brain turned back to Heart

III

Brain:

"We can battle this out but I warn you, there will be no victor."

Heart rebutted:

"What makes you think that?"

Brain:

"This body is being strained by its demons
The anger being released into our city is causing a mass panic
You have to calm down...."

Heat cut Brain off angrily:

"You have to trust in me and know that I react off impulse and intuition
I hardly ever worked without holding you dear to me
When will you understand this?
Maybe I have reacted too quickly at times but it is because of you
Your reaction time often slows the progression..."

Brain:

"Then we must work together."

Heart:

"What is this issue you've been speaking of?"

Brain:
"Because of our antics...this body has been lost
It doesn't know whether to have full faith in you or me
Remember when we first had our bouts?
The shootout between your comrades and my council
stirred so many emotions
We've been trying to handle them without you but..."

Heart:
"It doesn't *feel* right."

Brain:
"Precisely
Every move is cold for the body and everyone inside...
has been anxious and worried
Blood cells everywhere have been getting sick
due to the improper balance between chemicals
We have to get the city back on track and fight its demons."

Heart:
"Where are they?
Let's go get them!"
Brain:
"This is what I mean, you're moving too fast
I will plan and you will act
I promise to be quick
but it is a chess game so we must move strategically."

Heart let out a sigh and replied:
"Fine, let's plan this out
But STOP drinking so much!"

Letters to Eternity

But the key is to address those you hold dearest to you

Don't let them be a source of pain.

Cupid's Waltz in the Midst of Destruction

I

Most don't even know the extent of Love
that is placed on Cupid's scrawny
Hercules impersonating shoulders
His work goes beyond the Love between these hopeless romantics
The creator made him solely responsible for the relationships of all.

      He can't stand it.

You think God does all of this on his own?
Of course not, why else would there be angels?
Cupid, with the glare of the ripest apples shining in his eyes,
has multiple arrows for each and every relationship you can think of:
Arrows for heterosexual relations
      For homosexual relations
          For same sex platonic friendships
For different sex platonic friendships
      For family members...
For blood doesn't always equate to friendships.

Each arrow comes with certain sharpness
Dull arrows mean the relationship will not last longer than a few years
However, sharp arrows....

      Have you ever felt like someone is made from the same skin as you?

These relationships are bled from the same wound
Cupid's arrow is not linked to another
For these, he uses the same arrow on two skins so they are linked by the soul.

II

Today...
Cupid has a hangover
He drank too much love potion.

He's lying on his back
on his twin-sized cot
staring up at the ceiling wishing he didn't have to work
His eyes, half dead with the crust of a cloud in it
His ears, with an elves shape,
is deaf with headphones implanted
His valentine's red tunic still has residue from last night's meal:
Spaghetti and meatballs
The pasta just as twisted as he's feeling.

Today...
Cupid is going to half-ass.

But he's going to be smart about it.

He doesn't want to be responsible for putting terrible people together
for too long of a period
joining them with cuffs of God
So he gets off his cot, with his best "old-man" impression
Takes a swig of water from his post-hangover golden flask
sitting on his mantle piece
and looks for his arrows.

He grabs the dullest blunt arrows he can find
Hanging in the darkest corner of his room,
which is made of the thickest rubber cloud Heaven could find,
He does a quick set of morning wing stretches
and teleports from his chambers to the earth.

        The reason for his tiresome behavior?
        There is too much war on this planet.

With so much anguish and distrust,
people are moving twice as fast
making it harder for Cupid to hit his targets.

In the middle of a street, Cupid does his lazy waltz in slow motion
In between the frozen cars
with the passenger sides opening and closing every millisecond
People are moving rapidly and Cupid's catcher mitt eyes
can't catch a single person.

He takes his bow that is hanging from his back
Pulls out a few arrows from his pack
Dull with every color the rainbow had
and dropped like some backstabbing hues
Launches them all into one area at the same time
hitting me as I walked across the street.

What is the purpose of a relationship
if we are not chasing forever?
Whether we know it, understand it, do it purposely
or not...we enter every union of body, thoughts,
and values with the anticipation of forever
It is a chase that usually gets cut short...

Cinematic Mind: The Journal

I

As Dream Girl exited the second film,
She wobbled like a suitcase missing a wheel
She started to make her way down the theater halls
towards the final film.

On the walls were abstract paintings of family members
but she couldn't really make them out
The frames were golden plated ropes,
twisted Double Windsor knots,
bringing each color out.

The chandeliers hanging from the ceiling flickered
the further she walked until she ultimately made it to the end
There was a corridor leading to the right
But a table grasped her attention
with an eagle shaped vase
and an open journal.

> Every body holds a journal
> Inside this journal are secrets that a closet could never hold
> These secrets are written in the language of Enochian,
> A language only known to the angels,
> and it is embedded in a person's DNA.

II

This journal, battered and torn,
having the same age as the theater,
was signed with my name on it
The pages were magnetic
Being written by eyes as if they were the ink writing in it
They were translated upon Dream Girl's pupils cutting through them.

This particular journal held letters
to those that have either held a high position in my life
or continue to influence it.

> With every relationship is a reach for eternity
> It is the buck we all reach for
> Hardly ever do we reach it, but the journey...
> The journey is a story in itself.

Dream Girl opened to the first page and was immediately trapped in
Her eyes fluttered and then collapsed all together
Her body was transported into the letters

When Dream Girl opened her eyes again,
She was in an all white room with the same writings etched on the walls
There was a single chandelier hanging from the ceiling
and one of *Cupid's* stubbornly bold arrows on the wall
pointing to where she should start reading
With haste wrapped with confusion, Dream Girl began to read.

Addressed to the Keeper of Drama

I

We were about twelve when we met on your birthday
I still remember the sweet peach shaving fragrance
that captured the hairs growing in my nostrils
We were at your house
At this time we were both still timid
but your shyness didn't last too long.

Two years later you were already a crescendo of years
A dynamic I was waiting to experience
As with most girls in our city
Your sexuality had grown men's eyes jumping out of their sockets
and chasing you with a sprint only an orgasm could empower

Much like *Jennifer* from my high school…

You had become a temptress
Walk of a goddess
            Breasts of Athena
                    Legs of Shiva

but the stunning,

literally   freezing,

immaturity of the head of Medusa.

You had a knack for drama
and it wreaked of skunk life
being stoned to death by sewage.

II

I found that most girls had a similar background:

Intruders lurked their *kingdoms*
like bounty hunters with warrants placed over innocents
They are paid in pleasure to break in
and break IN young women.

They were avid fruit lovers
and picking cherries were their favorite pastime.

In your case, you knew your intruder
A friend of a friend
But on the night that he showed you a nightmare
with your eyes open
He wasn't very friendly.

This was only the beginning to what would become
your sexual prowess
You would become a bounty hunter yourself,
a *Trojan* to your seeds.

>Ironic how love that is stolen
>can quickly become love that is given freely.

Through the course of our teenage years
our off and on "friendship" slowly deteriorated
Your mouth was too pitbull
and your attitude grew tiresome
Plus I think there is a lesson that needed to be taught:

Sex will not bring you to a place
where sex will not be needed to get you through.

The sad truth.

Addressed to the Architect

The last time we had sex,
Your kisses tasted of apples sliced with a sharp sugar cane
A kind of kiss that alters worlds
They were gifts of pleasure dipped in a chalice of strawberries and cherries
wrapped by your stem tongue
There was an incomparable wetness that overflowed.

If the ocean had a body, it would be yours
A castle of salt water, shoreline tanned brick layered skin
Windows give birth to the sunrise in the sea of your eyes
The moon controls your legs tide, which opened for my wave
Tsunami language ruining the Japanese thriving city in your tongue
Hurricanes fluttering during dark periods,
I gave you a few, but many storm tears were self-inflicted by your own world.

You were my first taste of ecstasy
I never knew it had a bitter side
until you smacked my tongue with a spoiled flavor
An orchestra of paranoia held an echo between us ever since the first bite
A symphony
I tasted your symphony multiple times
My taste buds became seats for molecular musicians
beating their drums,
blowing their saxophones,
ripping their violins,
twice over
An encore.

Every phone call:
                              Where are you!?

Who are you with!?   *Who's voice is that!?*

                    Why didn't you pick up!?

I never understood why.
At this point, it doesn't even matter
Sometimes I wonder what would have happened
What could have happened if I swallowed your prickling pain
Swallowed the paranoia
Swallowed the fear that layered over your sweet inside
What would have happened if I swallowed you
and kept the bittersweet feelings that came along with it?

Would we have chased Heaven?

I wouldn't have minded that
But Heaven has so many gates to get past
My mind was too ill-mannered at the time
too green
too fresh
too rooted to the grass
too close to the seed
I was a baby trying to infiltrate Heaven's land
It was only right the guardians stopped me before I made it too far
We would've broke
But...there is no but
We weren't supposed to make it that far.

Sometimes castles are meant to be hotels
We aren't supposed to live in them
as much as we're supposed to visit
Our world was one to be visited
As ultimately, it didn't belong to me

Addressed to My Comrades

I

To my *comrades*,
As we stand in this dystopia
looking around at the rubble that we call, or they call, home
Let's remember why we live.

Let's remember that there is a city thriving under the skin
Not only within the wise,
But within everyone.

There is a city, a Zion, a Utopia, dying to pierce
the mannequin bodies that are on display in this society.

Our minds are set to "History Channel"
But we have to look deeper.

Comrades…look deeper.

II

There is a chemistry making up the minority being
Their body is the product of millennia
being passed down and mixed together
starting from the Pharaohs of Africa
slipping down like a reverse torch
touching the hands of European breeders and Spanish traders
Years of brewing by the great Alchemist,
the minority is a picture of a thousand colors.

Every person is complete with a chalk outline profile.

They say the arms carry:
the muscle of concrete with crack veins lacing it together
The wingspan of twin shotgun barrels
Switchblade fingers, rigid as prison shanks
Egyptian graffiti is carved into them like sleeve paintings
telling stories of street wars and odes to dead soldiers.

> The spine is an incomplete ladder of pride
> Countless bodies have dropped trying to build it higher
> But their Pisa backs can only go so far
> leaning like a crack fiend falling out of ecstasy .

The eyes are windows with varying shades covering the soul
which always tries to escape
You can tell if the soul is a king or peasant by its radiance
For instance,
The shades glow "gang" green for the simplest of beings: jealous souls
Pus yellow for the timid
Murder red for those carrying the devil's child in the womb of their hated

> The legs, with the strength of a million field slaves,
> walk amongst the wildest beasts
> They have the power of 400 decapitated horses
> and are bred to run any game Man can create
> Anything with a ball tickles the minorities' fancy.

III

> This dystopia
> is home base to the heavy metal drug lord
> playing rock under the listening nostrils
> A punishment sentenced during the 8th decade
> of the 20th century by the powers that be
> A punishment for the civil rights movements
> For the Malcolms, Martins, Hueys, Rosas, and Bobbys
> A punishment that has forever blanketed us for years to come

I heard one sniff could collapse a soul
and break a whole home crippled.

Now THAT is power.

IV

Why are you so angry, comrades?
What does this world owe you?

Why have we become so arrogant to believe
that this world owes us any privileges?

The anger towards our country needs to be obliterated.

I understand the past is a mixing pot of bloodshed and genocide
but what does dwelling upon it breed?

Unless you are willing to take arms, without gunfire,
change the world within you first
and then change the world within others
The stones of spite you cast should be planted back into the gravel.

We will reach forever,
but I'm afraid our views have divorced years ago
I no longer agree with the anger that once shadowed us.

The chemistry that created us is not law
We can change
I have
and will continue to.

Find the recipe for your evolution
That is true revolution.

Addressed to the One Who Hated Me

I

I remember the day so vividly
Funny,
You never expect to leave a day with such heavy frames
but when incidents happen, the picture remains in you forever.

So when I saw you leaving the building in cuffs
My eyes opened like a Venus flytrap
trying to attain all of the visual food.

Those are shackles on his feet...SHACKLES!

I didn't speak a word
None of us did
We simply watched you get escorted to the police station
and soon followed the scent of your innocence to that very building.

The pain of confusion came back
and nibbled away the Excalibur in my chest
as the officer said your crime with a deep-throat voice:
A crime that will never touch the page of any of my poems

II

Obviously you were innocent
But in this country, innocence is never a factor
Not when the prosecutor is White
and the defendant is a Latino.

Time consumed us into an absence
as you weren't allowed into the campus buildings
...or maybe time consumed me as my life went on faster
and yours seemed to move slower.

All I know is,
if I knew about the rage brewing in you before it erupted,
the segregation in our friendship race,
I would have tried to emancipate it
But I didn't.

All I remember reading in the message is: *"You didn't answer the call."*
The soldier on guard inside of me with its bruised shield replied:
"You never picked up the phone."

You asked me if I remembered when I told you
about all of my thoughts of suicide
We were 19 when those thoughts swarmed me like hornets
Soon after, it was you asking:

"The spirit is strong, huh?"

Years later you felt left behind
which is the case with most of my friends
as I have an awful habit of being drowned into myself
Sometimes it's hard for me to leave my own world
and enter the real one.

Growing up speaking the language of the ghetto
I often say *"I feel you"*
Years later, you would tell me:

"No...You don't feel me
You never will
You will never know the pain."

I understand that now
and though we both could have handled the last few years
in a better way,
I'm still sorry
for everything I didn't do.

When in defense, sometimes we say "I didn't do anything"
Not doing anything can be such a tremendous crime.

Addressed to My Confused Minister

I

To the confused minister in you
Let's pretend
Imagine that we hugged so hard that you fell into me
Into a place where stars forget to open their eyes.

Now,
Look around you
Look at the desolate desert dry land
with a crater the size of Zeus' heartbeat
It's pulsating…I think it needs something.

      What exactly?
I think it's waiting for you to find out
I heard that smiles must stretch daily
in order to bend upwards towards Olympus.

I haven't exercised mine in a while, could I borrow yours?
Whether it is an illusion or not,
it shines the color of happiness: radiating
Its magnetic curvature attracts…everything.

Forget about the crater.

Come to my desk and sift through the hundreds of poems
that will never experience the breath of new eyes
Each written in the ink of tear drops and unexplained thoughts
that leak out with them.

Take them. Strip yourself of your faith, wrap it around my written thoughts,
set it on fire, hold it up like a torch against the dark skinned sky
And wake the stars up for just a moment
I yearn for the burning feeling of security again
I wish the eyes of the sky would watch me again.

II

Are you still inside of me? Then come back to the crater.

Look in the middle and take note of the boy
sitting in the puddle of his own misery
Can you come down for a while?
Bring God's heart down with you
You smile like He used to
You speak to me like He would

I keep you at words length, so please pardon the distance
Please excuse the resistance,
the broken Babel tower of a wall between me
and anything that even seems reminiscent to Heaven
I fell once trying to build it higher
I don't want to fall again

Do you still have the torch?
Plant it in the middle of the crater as if you discovered a new land
Let it be the flag signaling to "Certainty"
that it can come back whenever it's ready

III

As we wait, come back to my desk
I will write you a poem. Or maybe a few.
I will write about the distant lands I've traveled in my mind
With exquisite detail, of course
I will tell you of the grand peaks I've climbed
I will explain to you the breeze that reminded me of God
every time it brushed my face and tickled my nerves
I will write about the letter I would have written you,
had I known you while I was there
I will write about the secrets I bought while shopping through Life
I will write about what I learned

I learned that nobody is different.

There is an eternal search injected into every vein
There is a yearning for hope
There is a hunger for protection
And we're all starving.

I met a lot of other travelers and they were all the same race
They shared the ethnicity of "irony"
They never realized the hope that they chased
made them latch on to false promises
They never realized that the defenses they put up for protection
came with weaponry that attacks even the innocent visitors
They never realized that they could be the very poison
they wished would never infect them.

It's sad.

They're not sad, but the idea of being able to travel a beautiful land,
even if it is only in my mind,
and merely notice the emptiness is a flaw that only Lucifer could have had.

I will write you a letter, would you like to read it?

IV

Dear you,
The one who impaled the crater with the faith wrapped poetry
Today, I sipped from the grand chalice of intoxication
It opened me up more than anything else in this world.

Last September, it killed my uncle.

Yesterday I cried, without tears, about the thought of failure
I forgot what currency looked like
For some reason, the two have become synonymous to me.

The day before, my sister cried, without tears,
because her eye sight has gotten worse
Her body shakes sometimes as her nerves slowly forget to do their job.

Sometimes, I cry thinking about the friends I've lost to violence
So selfish, right?
They're not even alive to be able to cry.

Sometimes, my sister cries, though she doesn't tell me
because she isn't allowed to work
or drive
or…have kids.
They're calling her handicap
Fuck them.

Sometimes, logic tells me I'm crazy
They're all normal, their faith is the engine driving their car through life
I'm still pushing mine.

I still remember the day I lost mine
The faith that is
It was in a chapel and I was in the middle of prayer
Maybe it was my demons but a sudden epiphany ran through me
Like a virus
Like a sickness
Like a plague
I cried the tears of a million newborns

There isn't a metaphor for a pain like that

It just hurts.

V

Has happiness come back to the crater yet?
Don't worry, it will
Just keep dressing your smile
with the latest galaxies the universe has to offer.

The hands of time have been in cuffs,
but liberation is soon to come
So patience is a must.

You thought I would forget about you
I won't.

When we let go of our hug and you fall back outside of me
I still won't forget.

You thought I was destroyed emotionally
Nothing destroys like the losing of one's faith.

But nothing heals like time
Time is eternal.

Time smiles like Autumn wind,
like the breeze of God's breath
the strength of Heaven's door.

So maybe you can keep your smile
I'll find mine again.

Addressed to God

Surprisingly, I speak of you often.

The story of your son's crucifixion has been penned into ink,
placed around the globe, and etched into my skin
Regardless of my acidic feelings towards you,
you are with me forever.

Understand my disbelief in you is not anger
as much as it is confusion
It really isn't that I *don't* believe in you
Rather, I appreciate the idea of you
but preach the gospel of "I don't know"
I dwell in the "why"
My eternal fight with "what if" leaves me bruised beyond belief.

As with most relationships, we have grown apart
Like scissor blades unable to come together
to cut through the steel block obstacles
We have become individual blades.

I found that losing faith
can black eye
a white skinned cloud
The outcome can be stormy
if not properly handled right after.

You heal the world the way you see fit
And I will in mine.

That is all.

Addressed to the Scion

To the Scion
You were my kingdom
My real kingdom

Before the civil wars

Before the nights of constant battles
on our lands and in our home

Before the collateral damage split friendships
and brought catastrophe to any messenger
or quiet enemies who tried to infiltrate

Before tears tsunami'd our faces
kidnapping any dry lands
splitting the Pangea on our bodies
flooding the country in our hearts
cracking the levees in our brains
raising the tide in our spirits
eradicating the steel connection between our souls
and the Milky Way galaxy rotation
of space between us

Two stars in different universes
trying to shine together
From a distance, I saw you
Light-years away

Before the orbit of gods were split
like an eclipse blinding the sun that the sky lassos
And the celestial fireflies that are embedded in the night
went out

Before we aborted the love we used to make
and the conception of it was just a spark
ignited by the flame of our breath touching

Before the bones that created our separate bodies of pride,
split up and joined together
mounting each other like some sexual hounds
and getting intertwined with the glue of hatred
creating an exo-skeleton that layered the outside of us

Before the kingdom became a glass house
An open house
Free for anybody to come in and sit on our sofa,
Watch our TV
Gain insight like a news station
set to the channel of "our business"
and giving the ability for anybody
to call in and give their opinion

Before the civil war erupted
and the spite in me
battled the anger in you
tearing the union in us

We battled like Heaven's legion on Hell
The same Heaven we were supposed to chase

We let it slip away
Like two headstrong race horses
losing their chariot
Our Love was inside of it
We lost it
It deteriorated in the midst of the battle

The chaos webbed around our bridge
The spider infiltrated it
The detonator went off

Before the grenade in us exploded
You were the first one I ever loved
You were my first queen
My first attempt at Heaven
and we let it get away.

> Dealing with you sent a message so chilling
> only the bravest are willing to read it:

Love is *always*

conditional.

Addressed To Herman

I don't play basketball but for now
I'll grip one
and try to palm it the same way you used to

I'll create your form for the jump shot you used to do
with your arms slightly arched after a fast break
Just for the moment I would like to recreate you

I want to stretch my arms out because you were always a bit lankier than me
and form that smile like you used to, so when your father looks up
and sees the slight wrinkles riddled on the right side of my face
maybe he'd envision you in me

If it was up to me, I would cut my chest open
Rip my rib out and play God in this fruitless Eden
forming you from what my heart left after your death

> They say your spirit still lurks,
> so let me commence in a reverse exorcism

Take hold of my hands and let me give you a jump start at life
Let me jump you back into your body from out the casket 6 feet
Just let me live like you until my life lets you live

> ...to make another jump shot

And as your memories silently spill into my mind
I can still hear the sadistic sounds of the shots going
POP!

> *POP!*
> > *POP!*
> > > *POP!*
> > > > *POP!*

> But it's only in my mind...

If God has the nerve to ask why
you tell him it wasn't your time yet!
You tell him the soundtrack to your life goes past track 18
If he says your story has ended, I'll tell him I'm a writer
I will tear the page of your death, because in my dreams it's still fiction
I'll create a new chapter...
I'll tell Him how your veins slightly bulged
when our homeboy got involved in drugs
and how you felt high with him
How you divulged the secrets in your eyes too painful to keep
so you branched out like trees
letting your heart lay out like the leaves pinned to them

You've become the broken rage which still plagues the young black youth
You are the truth stretched like a brutal penalty of death
You are the sands formed from demolished rocks
pushed with the currents of the sea
You are the lost thoughts burned of a polished book of poetry
You are the rubble of a kingdom crumbled with pearl and coral furnishings
and the cold air from a freshly put out furnace
You are the tears cried from a mother after 5 months becomes a miscarriage
You are an 18 year old still born
You are the wings torn from an angel who wasn't ready to fly yet
You are the soul taken out of a body that wasn't fully worn
You are the war for life that I'll keep fighting until God answers his door
and lets you come outside to finish yours

> And when our friends ask how you came back, you tell them!
> You tell them that your soul sees through my windows
> and you feel the world through the use of my finger tips
> You breathe with the air that I inhale,
> don't fail to say you come from my ribs
>
> You tell them!

You tell them that it wasn't your time yet
And every time the time gets confused
We'll place our hands on the hands of time
and become one with it
We will strip the power held within fate
Let's manifest this destiny intertwined

                    Let the rain drops splash both of our skin
                    as we stand on top your grave

Herman tell me, can you still feel me!?

Then try to understand…

When those bullets took your soul
out of the tranquil waters of my heart
the ripples you left never ceased

                    Years later I still can't find mine
                    so please tell me,
                    Please tell me…

you're resting

                    in peace.

(Film 3)

Chess Game With The Devil

Every player has their own game

If Darkness Should Fall

If darkness should fall, catching on to the tree branch of an eyelash
It would hang itself like a wet South Carolina slave
to the stubborn tears of my eye
I don't want to cry yet so I'll grip my emotions by the throat
and threaten to freeze them if they act out of order

Strangely, even I am surprised by the temperament controlling me
Enthralled by the fizzling of sparks before they erupt
I bottled them unintentionally
And so the internal civil war erupted, as the years became taxing

There is a certain distortion shadowing a Calm
The fortune telling of a Nagasaki bombing of self
An aftermath, Chinese knotted to the chest radiating as life adds adversity
We see it, ignore it, and blissfully exceed those who get caught in it

The day everyone became expendable was the beginning of the end
the terminal disease we were born with doubled in speed
Appointments with the Superior were called in early
The game of destruction has been slanted

Our inner demons aren't playing fair
They've banded together while we live certain separateness
If mine conquer me, I won't care to see theirs to help fight
Take the pain, embrace it, and see the beauty in darkness

There's a certain mystic in the night
I lay in shadows for there is a light somewhere creating them
When the time does come to play the game
I won't go easy.

Cinematic Mind: The Game

As Dream Girl erased her eyes out of the journal
the hallway began to disintegrate and vaporize
Peeling off like old wallpaper
Blowing away like dust on anything antique

In the newly formed room
I was there
sitting
Looking into the eyes of my shadow self
A marble table between us
with a chess board holding only the shadow's pieces

> I wasn't meant to play my demons
> Only dodge them
> To confront my temptations
> and confusions head on
> before they expanded

Dream Girl tried to walk over to me
but wasn't in control of her body anymore
Though she yearned to help me
All she could do was be there
while I faced them myself

I turned to her and smiled.

All I needed was for her to be there
Nothing less, nothing more
Having her be present while I faced my demons
was more helpful
She was more comforting
than she could ever know

With my *Heart* and *Brain*
my thoughts and impulses
Emotions and logic
back in sync
I was ready to play the game

The final film was being shot in front of her
as my shadow self moved the first piece...

From the Dusk...

I

Blood on his fingers drip slowly…

From Genesis times, there has always been a Devil's Knight
Shining a morning star bright
Dimming a sunlight glow
Dimming a son's light slow.

From Genesis times, he was the serpent's offspring
first tempting, then later through evolution
becoming the gremlin with a murderous psyche.

Today,
The hairy-skinned monster with gems cuffed around his wrists,
chains dangling like a loose noose around his neck,
sits at his throne in the four corner room of his whore infested bachelor pad
Dust falling off of him from the guillotine chopping of acidic snow
The same snow found in front of nostrils of mannequin stiff bodies.

It's his job to stiffen them up
To bring the Vulcan forth
Inviting the zombies to the four corners of the city pad
to exchange dead green men for their future demise in the shape of a rock.

This is the reason he moves in the shape of an L
He leads the lost.

II

The Knight was born during a broken sky
When the moon was highest and slept in the middle of the slit
3 gangsters dressed in Armani suits came bearing gifts:
A syringe,
A stack of money gift wrapped in a rubber band,
and the finest jewels.

The Knight
Born of a whore mother
Rested in a one-footed manger crib
in a broken down project building of any ghetto
two and a half decades before the great epidemic
Trickling into every decade after

He is the re-spawn.

He didn't cry at birth...

...He laughed.

His heart-wrenching chuckle burned fear into his mother
so much that she left the baby with the 3 gangsters
who raised him to breed madness.

As his peers were educated in the buildings that forgot books
and the *charcoal skinned teachers*
He skipped the nonsense
Excelling in the art of painting broken homes and sketching crowded blocks
his guardian archfiends were proud of his artistic growth
Of his ability to play architect and reconstruct homes
removing the foundation in which it once stood
His manipulation of picture perfect homes
by snapping only negatives was remarkable.

...Through the Dawn...

The Knight is made of all things acidic to the city air
Blood of a gangster, heart of mobster
Whether fiction or non-fiction, his book cover matches his pages
Attitude from the offspring of a television box and history
A Tony Montana split with Al Capone
A Luca Brasi merged with Frank Lucas.

These characters are boiled in the mixing pot
along with the crooked cops with the vortex fox smile
The city runners whose starting point is the same home he broke
The project infiltrations of Swat
with guns glistening with the shimmer of death in the moonlight reflection
The shadowy alleyway with the broken fiends waiting to be "fixed"

The Knight is the whole puzzle made of their pieces.

If he is the Devil's Knight
The rest of the pieces fall within his board
Without one, the game is tainted

If the crooked cops found a straight path
If the government ceased the war on drugs
Switching their players focus to the poverty war
The broke fiends would have reason to "fix" their communities
instead of themselves

Thus the (K)night would disperse.

...Til the Knight.

He rests somewhere in the city
after long nights of chopping product for the quivering noses to inhale
He usually leaves his host project tenement
like a temporary parasite
at around 3am...the devil's hour
He parks his rough calloused hand around a cold 40oz of Miller Highlife
and proceeds to the leather infested living quarters to live his own

Where the 52-inch screen illuminates the shadows on the walls
he sits at his throne, like a King
and slowly alters his perception
Every night, he plans the takeover of another street corner
while staring out of his large window cast over the world he distorted

He thinks he's God.

In some ways, he is a mini-version
with the conception of many children around the city
The doses of death he deals every day
The power to send a legion into any territory
and the people of his mini kingdom fearing his rule
He sits in the blissful Heaven of deception.

I saw him through the drug steamed mirrors
tempting me to ditch my home and relocate to his sanctuary
as he does with every young boy in the city
He looks for the break in the chain
so he can insert his pearly links.

So many souls are stuck in darkness
Shiny chains brighten them more than most would like to believe
Cars keep them moving in a world of stagnant living
The inner home is broken so the outer home is luxurious.

He tries to play family man,
sitting in the homes lacking a father figure
assisting with the bills when mother can't afford
Often the reason for my *eternal lament*
Being the reason for *Herman* and *Jarvis'* deaths
But because of my parents
my chain was stronger than sycamore
My chain hung around more than just my neck

      It was a piece of my body

At times, the Knight struck the impulses from my heart
Forcing the entries in the *journal of the thief*
stealing from those around me
creating an aura that my schoolmates could see
But it never broke me enough to reach my nerves
My thought process overcame the urge for riches
The urge for destruction of the very home I grew in.

      The Knight can be seen in the eyes of many
      But he almost never wins if the foundation within cannot be broken...

The Bishop...

Control one's beliefs and you control one's life
And so it seems there's a thin line between belief and brainwash.

It has been said that the human body is a sponge
ingesting every light, sound and bit of information
creating a Sun radiating, or regurgitating, back out
A human photovoltaic effect...so to speak

It isn't difficult to annul information or tweak what is in its mind
The great sculptors, hybrids of Donatello and Viacom
have positioned power to the Gepettos of the world
The media monstrosity or *Bishops*
that devours brain cells and replaces them with...

                                        anything.

The sculptors come in different phases, like water to ice to steam
Like the mind, body and spirit...a trinity of sorts
The great Bishop works through two phases
infesting through visual and audio
Two boxes offering different waves of information:
a television   and a radio
                    The ways in which we learn most
Parasitic cultivation of the nerves to strike
fear
            pleasure
                        and *hatred.*

I heard the only word you need to bring out our true hatred and fear is "terrorism"...

Manipulate perceptions and adjust them to the same channel
Bring control over the masses
Control their fear
Tailor what pleasures them
When the love of self is greater than the love of others
fear becomes the denominator and spokesperson for all

The Bishop knows this quite well.

Almost nothing the Bishop preaches through these venues is clear
The hidden agenda
is polluted by subliminal messages through advertisements.

> This is why the Bishop moves diagonally
> It keeps nothing straightforward.

Bishop indoctrinates the people's brains into thinking they have an issue
Disguising their antics as psychology and adding statistics to back it up
Feeding the empty all of the insecurities needed to vacuum their pockets.

> Bishop makes people feel empty
> They believe him.

...is Geppetto.

I saw him before...or should I say them
They're the ethnicity of everything
Skin splashing between powdered white and caramel brown
Suits, fitted over their demonic wings, the color of "dictator"
Their beady eyes have an archaic smile
Eyelashes flutter like weed whackers
Cutting through personalities
But the smile...the smile is of piranha teeth.

      Sinister smiles are the easiest to pinpoint.

In his boardroom office at the top of some building that pierces the sky
He sits at the father seat of a roundtable with his minions with generic faces
and mustaches worn similar to the British in 1775
The topic discussion is controlling those who live near distance to the Knight
with marketing schemes that should work like a new age *case of gods*

When the daily dosage is done
When the strings of Bishop are fused to the backs of the mindless
It brings them to a false mirror
to see the newly placed flaws the mind created
They repeat this oath:

      "I am of no substance
      I am worthless
      I have flaws that no one else has
      I am supposed to be godly in this ungodly world
      I am weak
      My power is minuscule
      Even if change is needed, there is nothing I can do."

      If everyone believes they have no power
      then as a whole, nobody does.

I was once a victim to the powers of Bishop
believing in the need of topical solutions for inner demons
The Devil's Bishop is intelligent in unimaginable ways
The teachings that I learned from the Buddhist and Christian ways
had a hand in straying me from false truths
You can't fix someone who isn't born broken
Inner hope is the only hope needed to survive.

Change won't come if we're all distracted
The Bishop's job is to distract
It can't win if it doesn't have the attention...

The Eulogy of Knights...

When the Devil's Knight falls and is taken by the opposition
His Pawn sings its eulogy by way of the Bishop
There is always a plan B
The Pawn's prayers have become a drug,
formulated into musical notes and injected into the ears
Beating the ear drums
Serenading the soul
Tearing the impulse away from the logic
Fueling the flame within
Hitting brains one Mp3 at a time
Keeping the Frankenstein shelled within the body alive.

...Breeds the Pawn's...

I

The Pawn is seen more than any other piece
He is a spitting image of the Knight
A breed sharing the likeness for flashy exteriors
The Knight splits the Pawn's chain and inserts his link,
dangles it from the neck, and glistens for all to see
This contagious effect is the bait.

The difference between them however,
is the Pawn is musically potent
The Bishop and Knight found a way to damage the players
without the use of drugs and alcohol
At least without them directly
There are no *clear syringes*
No *case of gods*
No triple beams and baking soda
No drug connect
All of these things become tapped into through indirect hands.

The new object of the game is switching the pieces
The new syringe is the microphone
The music is the drug
The distributor is the label
The connect is the store...or during post millennium, the Internet
What is better than a legal way of destroying homes?

Making a profit from it

II

As a seedling,
The rays of the Knight's jewels raised the Pawn
He is made to believe that the Knight is a King
which is the reason for the lack of a Prince on the board

As a child, he was rhythmically capable
and excelled in the English language
The Bishop took note, and his reaction was quite remarkable

He makes the Pawn believe that what he speaks
is not proper English and calls it slang
BUT instead of teaching him to speak differently
he promotes it and flings it to the ears of the future Pawns.

> *We love the language you speak*
> *but only if you choose to entertain us with it.*

In medieval times, the jester would entertain royalty
by dancing, singing, and juggling in bright costumes
The stage was lit with applause for their talents
Now these artists, with the potential of Dali,
are forced to dumb their expertise as the modern jester
Lay their "art" into wavelengths and push them into ears
But the fault is not theirs
The Knight raised them
For a piece of the sun, a piece of royalty
most would do anything.

...Influence.

From the Knight and the Bishop
to the Pawn to the player
The trickling domino effect becomes damn near genetic
As a child, I watched the Pawn
thus becoming one myself
His manipulation of the English language is so....amazing
Controlling words like Gepetto
The more intricate the wordplay
The deeper the tub my mind was brainwashed in.

I wanted the Pawn to tell me stories
Bring me into another world
I wanted to feel every gun explode

Every bullet rip into the flesh and asphalt
I could feel the injection of drugs
I could see the anguish of the world

Through the saliva of the Pawn
I felt every wave that destroyed homes in New Orleans

As a child, I couldn't always differentiate the real and fake
Fiction and non-fiction became one in the same
when all day, every day, the imagery and sound was embedded

It is easy to excuse the Pawns as just jesters and nothing more
But...
When they become something the player adores, a role model,
it becomes harder to tell the difference

Their lives resemble those around us
so we subconsciously imitate the message
If the stories aren't always straightforward,
like the Bishop's movements
how would we know which direction to move in?

Searching for reality was a part of my eternal search
along with the keys to a true belief system

Not all messengers are Pawns
But all Pawns are messengers

To be able to spot those under the control of the Bishop
is a talent that not all have been able to attain
Even the greatest of entertainers have fallen victim to Gepetto

When they stop relaying the message of the Knight
Pick up the pen and compose the artistry
that stains the Sistine chapel through music
They will become true prophets for my generation.

> *Their gifts are (w)rapped and distributed to children*
> *The wise know which ones to open...*

The Queen: All of One

I

She was the complexion of multiple shades
Baring the reflection of many ethnicities
A mixed breed of races
drawing from the pot that was *Wolf Ganged in America.*

But she isn't only from America
Her nationality is also split from the Latin Americas, Africa, Asia and Europe
Baring the body shape of all, yet in their own respective time
Beauty is in the eye of the beholder
Mine dilated in the palm that I held it in.

She was bilingual and her personality shifted to that of the language
From the food she ate, to her accent and traditions
She was open-minded in that way
Shifting by way of the seasons and years
She was a portrait of abstract colors and I was the frame.

Under the Devil's control, she was the epitome of distraction
Crawling underneath my skin and striking my impulse
making *Heart* takeover more than He should have
Whether it was lust or the imprisonment of love
Heart was disastrous during these times
Having an attitude shoot like a mouth full of firecrackers

II

Whenever my kingdom crumbles,
the insecurities fly around like some lost ghosts stuck in limbo
The Queen piece's thrown was shielded during devastation
While I cracked, she remained....or so I thought.

She would lie about past lovers,
and sometimes, even her present lover
thus gaining access to my domain
I open easily for Queens
It must be from the root tied between my sister and me
I feel for them.

> In this game, however, Queens can protect as well
> If not just as much, then more than the King could.

The Queen's original job isn't to protect only herself
But with so many kingdoms in opposition,
it becomes a habit to maneuver the board in every direction
In this way, she wouldn't get hurt
But in doing so, she risked hurting the pride of my castle.

> To destroy a man, don't attack his outer being
> Disassemble him from the inside.

Her multiple personalities kept me on edge.

III

Her attachment to other players was always obvious
It was as if her soul would attach to theirs even if only for a short time
Cupid would cuff them together, in a platonic manner first
Then romantically
From afar, I noticed, but kept the fire within silenced
because it wasn't my place to speak.

As we began to create our game, however
I expected her connections to cease
But when she jumped at the chance to protect the past
I felt the checkmate.

I was younger then
Couldn't understand my Queen having attachment to another
There was an idea that no one ever spoke of:
It is possible to love more than one person.

But I blame her territorial ways
If I was her territory only, then she must be mine
This love became more than something to be shared
We wanted to own it.

People are not meant to be owned.

In this tug of ownership
Our love became a battle
bringing collateral damage to anything around us
We started as rebounds from the past
Then joined teams
Then each other's property
It's quite obvious where we went wrong.

> *...the metaphor is breaking*
> *Let me break them down*
> *into the individuals they are...*

IV

Queen 1: The "confused minister"

A queen of great potential and spirituality
but lost in direction
Often preaching to me
while also trying to induce the sin of adultery
on me as well
Further spearheading the break already dwelling within me
She'll be the Devil's Queen only if I let her be...

Queen 2: The "keeper of drama"

I once thought she aborted life
so she could feel more alive
Maybe I was wrong
Perhaps she truly wasn't ready
The bridge we burned rekindled a bit
though I still haven't seen her
I hear she does well for herself
Came a long way from being the little deviant
I am proud she's overcome her demons.

Queen 3: The "architect"

I believe she was put in my path
so I could understand what it is that could boil my own blood
as the role I played between her and her real love
would happen to me down the line
Only in reflection would I see
that chasing what is already in the possession of another
will only bring turmoil.

Queen 4: The "scion"

We've been back and forth
in this boxing ring
since before our first round even started
I saw her in a dream
I saw her for a year
before I even spoke to her

When we finally broke
I was still shocked that she left me
basking in my own misery
…alone.

V

The list of queens goes on
All sharing me in common
a connection burrowed from a matter of lust
to burned friendships to false love
Making them one in the same
They are not the Devil's Queens
Rather, the devil in me is activated
if I pursued them with a certain burn in my eye
A burn that could disintegrate my connections
until they cease.

Castling (Where the King and Rook meet)

There is no complete way to disrupt the Knight
nor the Bishop
nor the Pawn
The fight never completely ends
It is a throbbing war surgically impaling the Heart
and thrusting the Brain over and over
like slaves receiving lashes

...just because they are alive.

Where we fail to climb over
the King and Rook will exceed

Lust.

envy   addiction
obsession   gluttony

Ideas that lynch moderation by the thread
for the constant need for something whole
The rejection of a slice for the loaf
A permanency in hunger with a full stomach

The Bishop plants the seed
The Knight waters it
The Pawn grows from it
The wrong Queen will provoke it

The castle builds inside
castling in the yearn for material objects
or even the reach for success
matched with the failure of retrospect
for anything already accomplished

Ungratefulness

Ungratefulness is an infection
passing through most humans without any thought of sickness

II

The lock
burrowed within the lust
rejected by the degrees of separation
lost in the midst of war between Heart and Brain
will lock up insecurity
build the spine back together
bring understanding to the fly
and calm the chess pieces.

I have to understand my own demons
Recognize the times that I have lost
and be grateful for the wins as well.

The final chess piece
resides within.

When The Castle Crumbles,

The Kingdom Rebuilds

After Herman's funeral, my mother took me to church
I cried in my pastor's arms as he read the scripture on my arm: Galatians 2:20
He said "Hakim, Herman's dead."
Then with a slight smile, he brushed a tear off of my cheek and said:
"But YOU'RE still alive."

Kingdoms

"...my inner kingdom was shattered"

One bullet
     Two bullets
         Three bullets
            Four
As each second passes another kingdom hits the floor.

Bloody rubble
     Cold caskets
         Kings clashing
           Guns roar!!

As radiation hits our paintings, they are melted to the core
Libraries become furnaces up in flames, furniture burns, unfurnished
Picket fences and gates blurred with explosions

         Screams from ghosts can be heard!

Skeletons that were once trapped in closets are free to be
Making home in their prior habitat taking refuge in their old bodies

      Hearts that were once sewed to sleeves like team patches pack up
      and bleed its way back into the open rib cage gate
      it was once packed in

Pride is packaged,
wrapped by what little dignity is left
and shipped off by way of humiliation and anxiety.

Secrets seep deep into pores
mutating castles into the imperfect kingdoms they truly are
The silver tint of cloudy doubt becomes more reasonable by the minute

Have you ever witnessed a castle crumble?

As all hope comes tumbling down
what happens to our crown when oxidation takes effect?
After years of battle, still hold your weapon to its highest extent.

FUCK soldiers!

We fight more like gladiators in the form of modern day man
Kill all generals who infiltrate, exterminate their goals *AND* their plans!!
And each and every individual throne
that feels the need to break down your own
We own the land
      We own the earth
          We own everything
              This world
                  We are man!!

Bloody bastards, every last one of them!

With their own agendas, ulterior motives
See past their bullshit
they pull shit, pop shit!

I remember when I first attained my kingdom
I painted all over it: roses with my mother's name,
Bible scriptures,
Even the Devil earned his place on my walls
My windows with brown tints, squinted till the glass was replaced
MY eyes, *MY* place

      Embrace your kingdoms!

Because so many people lost their sense of royalty, look in the mirror
We are not simply kings and queens fighting for our crowns
We are worth so much more
We are Gods with rhythm,
We are the earth
We are everything and nothing at all

Do you know why skeletons get trapped in closets?

The inner secrets of our soul are wrapped in the flesh you were blessed with
Civil wars within ourselves
Wars between allies we once had a union with
We are more than just kings and queens

LOOK IN THE MIRROR!!!

Most don't even realize they are more than just royalty
We are worthy for more than just crowns
With all of this blasphemy, we have forgotten:

We are kingdoms…

    …and when others try to infiltrate our territory
    We have a right to defend it

    So defend your kingdom
    Until the walls fall in...

Cinematic Mind: The Exit

When the game finally ended
When I finally came to the realization
that I had already beaten my demons
Dream Girl found the strength to move again
She could leave me.

My shadow self slowly vanished into me
It won't go away...

But that was never the point.

The point was to be able to face my demons
                 and if necessary
have an open ear to be there with me

          My Dream Girl

II

I got up from the marble chess table,
with the broken pieces laid across it,
walked over to Dream Girl
and pointed to the door straight ahead of us
It was time for her exit.

As she turned the knob, dust began to fall from the ceiling
Chandeliers in the next hallway began shattering
and falling to the floor
The theater was crumbling into itself
The *Fly* on the wall had vanished
The painting of the war had a layer of black
painted over it

The poems that were etched into the wall were gone
The journal was torn into pieces
thrown into the vase on the table and lit on fire.

Dream Girl began to run through each hall leaving me behind
in the destruction of this theater of scattered memories
in the rubble and ash of a phoenix
that would rise from it
The rebirth of life with the chance of righting wrongs

As she made her exit
I was left to be able to find gratefulness
and rebuild from it.

Sin.

The cloud in your eye swallowed me a crescent moon full
Something was definitely peculiar between us
like the way your eye dilated a summer thick
on every occasion I'd spring into your peripheral
The pool of your lust was hard to swim in

I noticed it from the conception...

and was tempted since the first time
that Saturn ring orbited off your finger
Tales sold itself off your tongue
like a prostitute's corner tune
about faith and your troubled marriage

For a while, I sat in the choir you *ministered*
I began to let my lustful body bathe in your secrets
while my thoughts smoldered us a bedroom

I thought I could learn the snare of your music
from the inside

      While he wasn't home...

You could teach me the violin of your nerve,
the snap of its curve

      While the kids slept...

We could breathe the crackling fire of a drum
when I lean into you

      The same as when you hugged
      and fell into me

We'd love the *crater* full
Fuck a cloud's bolt out of *Zeus' heartbeat*
hanging the smile in your home
on to the mantelpiece in the underworld

       And when he finds out
       When he hears of our deed

It'd burn a phoenix in his chest
So eternal
So internal
The kids would perish into the ash of him
but never rebirth

Sometimes demons win...

        ...but sometimes, the ground we walk
should never let them stand a fuckin' chance

I said I wouldn't forget you
      But I did.

I could never give room in the hall of my sanctuary for a sin that deep.

Daydreaming

"I slip into another world..."

My son said to me:
"You didn't wear one
and now you have thoughts of being the Trojan Horse to me
Infiltrating.

Indeed that brain of yours bathes in a tub of lies
being brainwashed to the allure of false freedom
You think destroying me before I tear through this dimension is the answer?
You couldn't be more wrong father
For while you were busy being *architect*
I was building myself from the ground up

Let me explain...

Your spite and mother's insecurity are a whirlwind together
In this morgue of plebians, I will remain prince
The anger I extracted from you
mixed with the art of her...deadly!
Do you have any clue what kind of an artist I will be?
DO YOU?!
There's gasoline in this here earth
My paintbrush is going to light it on fire
My pencil will design a soliloquy that will be home to classrooms
and minds around the country.

Her love for art and yours for poetry will fuck twice over
conceiving so much talent in me
You're not ready to be a father
But are you ready to abort a future inspiration for change
in the very community you grew in?

Roxbury

Nah, I don't think so
You're stronger than that.

Ball that fist up, ya hear?
Write about it like you used to
We will be a weapon to reckon with
Just PLEASE give me a chance!

You got one; I deserve one too
Father remember,
The only idea greater than your yearn to be a writer
is writing a new life into the very existence of this world
The ONLY time you will ever see yourself pure again
is looking into the eyes of your child during birth...

But in the meantime, stop fogging your mind
She's not even pregnant
Though it's funny how the scare of new life
makes you recognize the prize just lingering in your own
Take advantage of this time
You need something to pass down when it's really my time."

When I picked up the phone call
The architect told me she wasn't pregnant
I leaned into my bed a little harder that night
Pondering the future
I wondered if I'd make my child proud.

The Five Years Later Haiku

...after our buzz was blown.

Gerald said to me:
"The reason I got away
is because of God".

My Mother

My mother has four odd eyes
   With paint brushes for lashes
    Canvases for pupils
      Eyelids proportionately enclosed
      around the images
      of her four babies

      Paintings
     Squared in detail
    resembling sixteen Sistine chapels
   all in the intricate Vatican of her soul
    With a heart split like embers
  Flaming to the crackling sparks of our smiles
whenever our laughs hammer into the concrete coldness of the world
   she rode us in on with the saddle of her womb

    Her womb
With walls made of the tissue
she once soaked her father induced tears with
almost became my tomb
as my early depression forced my suicidal tendencies
making my baby hands grab the closest rope it could find,
the umbilical cord, wrapping it twice around my neck

I wanted to hang from the crooked liberty statue of pain
before her flame went out and pushed me through
I was so scared

     But my mother,
    after delivering two other sons,
    like the ocean does every dawn
     as if it mothered daylight,
   She sang "*You are my sunshine*" ever so gently
   Like a secret only the illuminati could know
  The relationship between a mother and her children
    is a secret society you have to be born into

Only no secret handshakes
        No hidden messages
                or steps
                      or strolls
                            or chants
                                or poems
Just framed faces in her eyes
and the words "*I love you*" draped across the sky
as if she stole God's pen
and leaked its ink into the atmosphere

I drown in her chest when she hugs me
getting stabbed by the Poseidon trident rib cage while it swings open
to catch me whenever I free fall into the sea of life

        I would never be too old to be called "mama's boy."

Never too proud to let her kiss me in public
while the rest of the world Cyclops gaze at the cord
that I once tried to kill myself with
and how it seemed to never be broken between us
Even in the days when I'm too stubborn to get on the stand
and testify the trials I have witnessed
I'm still too scared to be judged
But if I would let anyone do it…

        ..it would be her

with the godly cloak of wisdom she sports
like knowledge is her only fashion
and the gavel fist of passion she strikes down with so much authority

My mother is not like my father
She's not a *shooting star*
She's more like the space that stars travel through
for without it, how could suns shine?

They'd just be a black hole of their own existence

All soldier and no throne
        All heart and no soul
                All pulse and blood
And thought
And logic
And instinct

                But no *love*!

And we need that

I needed that.

Her District

...my relationship with the District of Columbia

She moans like police sirens. Blue and red spewed from her vocal cords when her leaky legs open wide for the public. I'm fairly new to her district so I follow the lines of her veins like subway tunnels in New York. They're surprisingly clean, unlike the ones of my former lover. Train-like blood flows to the minute, never really skipping a track like a "professional" dope fiend. And for this, I nicknamed her Columbia. Nothing is really native to her, just imported for the sake of capitol.

I remember the first time I saw her. It was in the funeral cold month of January and her
stepmother, winter, dressed her in all white.
She was still attractive.
As time flowed, her cherry blossom cheeks started to glow cupid pink in the springtime
weather. She was beautiful in that way, changing colors like a timed roulette-rainbow.

She has her dark periods. Sometimes they were very dark. Her bipolar temperament led people to only deal with her during her light periods; the times when business and politics overshadowed her hoodlum ways. Simply crossing the street would make Columbia twist and bend like a pretzel. One minute you were on a clean slate, the next you would be looking over your back hoping she wouldn't twist *you* as much as she is.

Her hair flowed of brittle rocks through ocean waves.
There were too many textures to fully recognize a single race within her.
It was like driving on a street with all kinds of damages on one side, and smooth
grounding on the other. She was mixed in that way.

She never could keep a man, usually marrying for about four years at a time switching according to the presence of the alpha male with the stars spangled in his actions.

She was full of hypocrisy.
I wondered how she could step down from a stoop,
walk past a man finding a home on the street
treating the sidewalk as a bed,
and then speak on poverty abroad.

I was divorced from Columbia after her cheeks bloomed cherry,
as children began to gather at parks smiling as if their imaginations
were running loose into the wild. It was during the graduation month
when dreams started knocking on doors asking owners if they were ready
for tomorrow. My mouth tasted of watered-down sweet nectar.
As I boarded the train to leave, I took one last look back at her
and smiled so hard the wrinkles in my lips reached my ears.
She smiled back.

There was an umbilical cord of respect that stretched between the both of us.
We'll never truly be apart.

Learning to tear the Cocoon

There are a string of words entangled within me like a beehive
All instrumental wind chasing stubborn fellows preying to own air
Hoping to chew through every oxygen atom they can graze their atoms on
The arranging
and rearranging
of 26 letters that will coerce
being hitched into stanzas
till they morph worlds

> The first poem I ever wrote…like EVER
> was in high school, about my sister
> This is why she always gets the credit
> for every letter that unscrews its sanity
> from my tongue

Being behind the 4th wall of stage
although nerve quaking a magnitude of 10.0
The aftershock is enough to break any shell cocoon
I may ever be in

I've always spoke of poetry
like it was an old friend from down the street
As if these words weren't MY words
As if I preyed to their omniscient aura
Always looking for something to believe in
instead of believing in myself

This hive of words has only been the variable
In leading me to the place I should've always been
Not blaming God
        or gangs
        or the country
        or women
        or alcohol
        or any other thing for my insecurity

_____

The personification of my Heart and Brain battling
is just an abstraction of the real battle a lot of people go through
Not acknowledging that logic and intuition need to work together
Breaking my timidity would require me to be impulsive
Learning to tear my cocoon through writing
gave me balance

After running for so long
It finally finds its resting spot
Takes off its cool
and begins to build itself together
for the first time
It finds a face, and sculpts it to resemble her
Grabs his chest and molds it into itself
Alchemist opens up the little bulb
Places a one watt of a soul in
and presses on

It flickers a few times...

The Alchemist turns it off
Unscrews the bulb
Places it gently into the *Not Ready* section of *Elsewhere*
Picks up another bulb and screws it in

He presses on...

The sound of light surges through the Heavens
Bustles into the clouds and impales Earth
The light has brand new set of wings with it
with a thread and needle...

Hearing Sight

I thought I heard the sound of her smile
or maybe it was the sight of her words
Something about the translation of her body language spelled

Happiness

On Christmas morning
there may not have been a new messiah born
but the *nerve of darkness*

or

Her Multiple Sclerosis
finally had a light on it

I heard the wings being stitched back onto my sister's back
as she showed my family the ultrasound
The sound of her baby
I don't know if she heard my *Heart* smile
but it did...

Loud.

Epilogue

What I Do Believe

...She was searching for my conviction- my beliefs,
and my reasons to be

I believe in balance
I believe if you can love, then you can hate
I believe hatred can be used for good
I don't believe in God
I believe that Jesus Christ's story is beautiful
I believe that we should all strive to be like Him
whether He is real or not
I believe everyone has the right to make a judgment
I believe everyone has the right to change that judgment
I believe everyone can change
I believe everyone deserves a second chance
I believe in forgiveness, only if a person is apologetic
I believe romantic love is conditional
I hope someone changes my mind
I believe in gay marriage
I believe some people are truly made of hatred
I believe that because of this hatred, war is sometimes necessary
I believe war is not only made of guns and bloodshed
It can be a clash of ideas
I believe everyone learns differently
I believe everyone is unique
I believe everyone is similar in more ways than they like to admit
I don't believe in karma
I believe karma can be an indirect way of wishing the worst
on someone who has wronged you
I believe bad things happen to great people
I believe bad things happen to terrible people
I don't believe in psychics....yet
I believe we should accept the world as it is
and then change the world to what it could be
I believe that if I bring more smiles than tears
then I must be doing something right
I believe the human brain is powerful
I believe the brain distorts what reality really is for everybody
I believe my parents saved my life
I believe my brothers saved my life
I believe my sister saved my life

I believe Hip Hop saved my life
I believe poetry saved my life
I believe Christianity saved my life
I believe Buddhism saved my life
I believe everyone has the right to his or her own beliefs
as long as that belief does not bring destruction to others
I believe in people
I will always believe in people
I believe that we need more faith in each other
I believe in equality
I believe in the love of all people, all races
I believe the root of evil is the love of ignorance, not money
I believe this world is too dirty to clean
I believe that is not an excuse to not try
I believe that forging the future
will not be accomplished by dwelling in the past
I don't believe that I will change the world
I believe that I will change many worlds
I believe that I have already changed the world within others
I believe fear controls more than respect or money ever could
I believe two wrongs don't make a right
I believe we all have demons similar to the *liquid demon*
I don't believe I should completely cut out alcohol, lust,
or any other thing that I may be a glutton for
I believe I should keep a discipline
for if I have to completely stay away from it, ultimately, it still controls me
I believe all of the women I have dealt with are beautiful in their own way
I believe there is another demon in me that yearns to be alone
and because of it, relationships will never reach forever
I believe everyone is meant for something
even if it is small
I believe that every religion has something in common
They all want to make our existence a little easier to deal with
They all want to give hope
They want to give comfort
I do not believe in organized religion
But I do appreciate them
I believe we should all find our own way to make life better for the next
I believe writing is my way
I *still* believe...

To Catherine

To the young girl whom I've never had the pleasure of meeting
who wrote me a letter letting me know how much I've influenced her
to keep on writing…

        All of these words are for you.

I imagined you into the "Dream Girl"
feeding on every word like sustenance
That letter was the first time I ever felt like anybody
has ever really uncovered their jar
and poured my thoughts
making their eyes erect like an audience
cheering to the concert between my letters

        A concert only I was supposed to know about

So in retrospect
After four years of review
I didn't really influence you as much
as you did me

Thank you
I hope you never stopped writing.

..but the search never ends..

"You were crucified with them...nevertheless you live"

In the end,
the scab of night peeled off the wounded sky
revealing a growth in its flesh
A brand new tower
rose from the ashes of a broken castle
Twisted its construction until its tip formed a key
unlocking the space of time
through a distorted galaxy of past
The universe door opened with a blinding light

and when it ceased

When the light minced itself into the present
Herman and Jarvis revealed themselves, both smiling
They said it was never them who died
I did.

But it's okay now
With every search comes a chance for rebirth
I've earned mine
They never stopped believing in me.